THE NEGOTIABLE
GOLF SWING

THE NEGOTIABLE

JOSEPH LAURENTINO

GOLF SWING

*How To Improve
Your Game Without
Picture-Perfect Form*

A Mountain Lion Book

ISBN 0-9770039-2-2

Jacket and text design by Bob Antler, Antler Designworks

The Negotiable Golf Swing is available at special quantity discounts for use
as premiums and sales promotions, or for use in corporate golf outings.
For more information, please contact:

NEGOTIABLE GOLF
1019 Ft. Salonga Road
Suite 10-180
Northport, NY 11768-2209
www.joelaurentino.com
info@joelaurentino.com

Realize your full golfing potential.

In Memory of
VINCENT A. LAURENTINO
1934—1995

Contents

Preface

n 1974, at the age of 12, I became a golfer. My dad introduced me to the game and gave me my first set of clubs, a ladies' set of Northwestern irons. I still remember the excitement of getting that first set. By eighth grade in junior high school, I was playing and practicing frequently, had developed some skill, and was good enough to be invited to play on the varsity team at Centereach High School on Long Island, New York. I played on the team in eighth grade and high school. By the 11th grade I played in the number one spot. We had a good golf team and went three seasons without a defeat.

Through my junior high and high school years, I worked at Spring Lake Golf Course, a local public course, where I could also practice and play for free. My dad was my only teacher, but by the time I was 15, he realized he had taken me as far as he could and suggested that I seek help from a professional. I took a couple of lessons from Lorin Hawkins, the pro at Spring Lake. But I didn't want to take lessons or practice; I just wanted to go out on the course and play. My memories of those days are of tips like "Keep your head down," "Drive the legs," and "Slow down your swing." By the end of 11th grade, my interest in the game started waning. I was more interested in hanging out with my friends, being cool, and talking to girls. It showed. My golf game suffered. I slipped from playing the number one position to playing the number three and four positions on the team. My ego was bruised, but golf just wasn't that important or exciting to me.

After graduation, in the fall of 1980 I was enrolled in the Professional Golf Management program at Ferris State University in Michigan. The program was designed for students to receive a

Bachelor's degree in business, with a minor in a golf program. The credits for the golf-related courses, along with internships at golf courses around the country, were applied towards PGA membership, education and experience requirements that are necessary to become a PGA Professional. I had long hair, wore a black leather jacket, and had two earrings in my left ear. I was a real rebel; in fact, I was the only guy on campus who wore an earring (Ferris State is in the conservative midwestern part of the country) and I looked much more like a rock musician than your stereotypical golfer working towards becoming a PGA Golf Professional. The golf program began at Ferris State in 1975, but was still a small program in 1980, with less than 100 students in it. More or less, the guys were all very conservative in their attitudes and dress, with the little animal logos on their polo shirts, basically dressing and acting the role of future golf professionals. I'm a friendly and outgoing person, one who could talk with anyone, but I was very uncomfortable among this group and felt like a misfit. By second semester, I dropped out of the golf program but continued studying for the business degree.

After I dropped out of the golf program, I put the clubs in the closet and didn't care if I ever played again. There was no way I wanted to become a golf professional at a country club. I spent the rest of my college time doing what I had liked to do in high school: hung out with friends, dated girls, and played my drums in college bands. My dream was now to become a musician: a rock and roll star.

After college I returned home. But making a living as a musician wasn't something that I had enough talent or drive to do. I was a mediocre drummer at best. I hung out in a local music studio, saw how much better those guys were than me, and realized that even they couldn't make a living just from making music. Over the next few years I had various jobs, selling audio equipment and working in bars and restaurants. At the age of 27, I was still living at home with my parents where I was surrounded by the influence of golf. My dad loved the game. He played as much as he could, going to the range whenever possible, practice-putting in the house, hitting balls into a net in the garage, reading and studying every golf instruction book and magazine, and watching every golf television broadcast. He was a low single-digit handicap player who had a true passion for the game, though some would refer to it as an obsession. One day I was talking to my dad while he was hitting balls into the net in the garage and asked him if I could hit a few. It had now been nearly eight years since I had even hit a ball. My dad saw a spark in me and bought me a set of knock-off Tommy Armour irons. Working in the bars at night afforded me the opportunity to have my days free, and I started playing and practicing during the day. My passion for the game quickly returned. Within a year, I was practicing a lot, sometimes going to the range and hitting as many as 500 balls in a day. The next thing I knew I was as obsessed with the game as was my father. I was reading books and magazines, watching all the tour events, practicing, playing, and even putting in the house. As they say, the apple doesn't fall far from the tree. But still I had not sought advice from a golf professional; instead, like most golfers, I thought I could figure it out on my own. I felt I was only a tip or swing thought away from finding the magic solution. I also quit playing the drums around this time.

In the next few years, I reached the point where I was consistently shooting in the mid 70s and playing in some local amateur events. In 1994, I decided to leave the restaurant and bar business. I didn't know what I wanted to do, but I knew I was truly passionate about golf. I decided to again explore the idea of becoming a golf professional. I took a job at Indian Hills CC, a private country club on the north shore of Long Island, working as an apprentice making $7.50 an hour, and eventually became an assistant professional in the latter part of that same year. The following year my dad died of a sudden heart attack. As it is for many children who lose a parent, it was a devastating time for me. Because golf was such a strong reminder of him, I struggled to get myself to play. In a way the game made me very sad. The following year, happier times were upon me when I married my wife, Christine, who has been a great support system for me and my career in golf.

AN IMPORTANT STEP

In 1997 I completed my PGA schooling and became a member of the PGA. That same year I was awarded the position of head golf professional at the club. I had come full circle since I had decided that I didn't want to be a golf professional at a country club and quit the golf program in college. But even from my start as an apprentice, my true dream was to play golf for a living, to be a PGA Tour player. I was working six days a week, but I always made time to practice and play. I stayed on the course until dark almost every day of the season.

Maturity brought the motivation, determination, and focus that I didn't possess in my younger years. Now, improving and becoming the best I could be was an obsession. Every winter from 1993 through 2001, I was very fortunate that the members at my club raised money for me to play on one of the many professional winter tours in Florida. For me, a typical day in Florida, when not playing in a tournament, was to get up early in the morning to exercise and stretch, hit balls for a couple of hours, play 18 holes of golf, hit some more balls, and go back to the gym at night. No going out at night or socializing, just a 100% focus on golf and improving my game.

The season at my club is from March through December. At the club, I was doing the things golf pros do: merchandising, scheduling, supervising, handling tournament operations, and giving lessons. I also played in the local professional tournaments in the New York metropolitan area, something I still do today. During these eight or so years, I sought help and advice for my game from some of the most well-respected golf professionals in the country. I have read nearly everything there is to read on the subject of the golf swing. Of course, I was also giving lessons at this time. I changed my swing theories frequently, many times trying to apply the same ideas I was working on in my own game to my students' games. Some of my students got better, some got worse, and others stayed the same. In retrospect, I think many of those early ones deserve a refund.

As far as my game was concerned, at the end of every Florida trip, I looked at my game objectively. I really wasn't improving. Although I was able to shoot in the 60s at my home course, my game was very inconsistent and I couldn't produce any of these low scores in tournaments. This was in part due to my struggle with the mental side of the game when competing in tournaments. Many times I felt like I was making a breakthrough, applying some different philosophy or methodology to my golf swing, but the improvements were always temporary and my ideas and approach to the game were constantly changing. So much time was put into improving, but the results were just not forthcoming. At times all of my efforts felt like a waste of energy. I came to the sad realization that I was not going to be a tour player and make a living playing golf. Instead I set my sights on being the best golf instructor I could be. But first I had to find a theory I could believe in and stick to.

MY EYES OPEN

Sometime in 2001, I decided to take a lesson from Michael Hebron, a well-known, respected, and nationally ranked golf instructor. The golf course that Michael worked at was only 10 minutes away from my club. Although I had sought the advice of many other golf professionals, I avoided Michael because I had heard that he had a very technical approach to the golf swing. But I soon found out that he was not overly technical. I now saw things in a different light. Much of Michael's focus was on the learning process, the state of golf instruction and its downfalls, and the science of the golf swing. These ideas were a turning point in my teaching, as well as in my own game. Over the next couple of years I only saw Michael about two or three times a year, but I studied his theories in depth, and also read the material that influenced him. I can't emphasize enough Michael's influence on me and my teachings during this period. Over the next few years, my thoughts and theories on the golf swing and golf instruction started to change. Until this point, my thoughts had been, at best, muddy and cloudy, but now they became clearer.

ANOTHER TURNING POINT

In the winter of 2003, my son had his first birthday and I decided for the first time to not play tournament golf in Florida. It just wasn't as important to me as spending time with my wife and my son. With two months off, I wanted to spend time with my family and do something to occupy some of my free time. Deciding to take up the drums again, I took some lessons. I was fortunate to have the opportunity to take the lessons from Dom Famularo, a world-renowned drum educator, who has written books on drumming and motivation and who has conducted clinics all over the world. He possesses a very positive attitude, one that is infectious to those around him. The first time I met him, I was envious of his positive energy. After my first lesson, we left his drum studio and Dom took me to his office on the top floor in his house. Since we were both instructors, we talked about how to help others learn and improve their skills. As we spoke, I told him I was thinking about writing a book on golf instruction and had formulated some ideas for it and for a website. He asked if I was taking notes and I told him they were in my head. He strongly suggested that I start writing down all of my ideas. He was very encouraging about the prospect of my book and a website, and I left his office that day inspired to try to do something great with my ideas. It was another turning point for me.

During the next couple of years, I took many notes. Once I had some structure to my theories, I started to write. During this time, I also studied the mechanics of the golf swing further and focused on observing how people learn. Many of the things I learned came from observing the golfers I worked with, myself as a drummer, and my young son learning new motor skills.

I know that I do have something new to offer golfers. I've seen it in the improvement of my own golf game as well as in my students' games. I know that my ideas can help golfers of all levels improve. I've had a long and personally fulfilling journey as a golfer, golf professional, and golf instructor ever since my father passed on his passion for the game of golf to me. Now I want to pass on to you the knowledge that I have gained on that fulfilling journey.

Acknowledgments

There are so many people I need to thank for their help and support with this book. First, my wife, Christine, who continues to be my biggest cheerleader and whose love and support was unwavering during the many hours that had to be sacrificed for this project. My children, Sophie and Quinten, who are constant reminders of what's important in life. My brother, Vince, for his invaluable feedback and guidance. The ownership, management, staff, and membership of Indian Hills Country Club for their continued support and encouragement.

I also want to thank my literary agent, John Monteleone at Mountain Lion Inc., for believing in me and my ability to write this book, as well as for guiding me through every aspect of the book publishing process. Roger Masse, for his collaborative efforts and editing skills, all of which helped shape a manuscript into a book, one that I'm proud to put my name on. Susan Brooks, for her copyediting skills and polishing the manuscript. Phil Franke, for the enormous effort he put into the visually stunning illustrations. Bob Antler at Antler Designworks for designing a book with such visual appeal. Photographer Robert Walker, for his skill and efforts on the interior photographs in the book. And Jim Lennon from Brenner/Lennon Photo Productions for the cover photography.

In addition, I would like to thank the many golf professionals who personally contributed to my education as a golf professional, as well as the many authors of golf instruction books that preceded mine. I want to especially thank PGA Professional Michael Hebron, whose coaching philosophy influenced me and brought me to the point where I could write this book.

ing me to write this book and for entrusting me with their golf games. I've learned so much from all of them.

Introduction

Jack Nicklaus's flying right elbow. NEGOTIABLE.
Ben Hogan's flat arm swing. NEGOTIABLE.
Arnold Palmer's helicopter finish. NEGOTIABLE.
Curtis Strange's floating head. NEGOTIABLE.

Each of these idiosyncratic mannerisms, from Nicklaus's elbow position at the top of his swing to the movement of Strange's head in his backswing—although indelibly distinctive of the respective golfer—nevertheless functions as an integral part of the consistent, repeatable swings of these legendary golf champions. They are characteristic of the individual player, but not damaging to his performance.

They are negotiable. That is, they are part of a compatible arrangement of the many permissible alternatives that, while not conforming to the computer models of the perfect golf swing, can still function very well to get the job done. These negotiable elements, from the setup to the finish position of your golf swing, represent the subject of this book. By identifying and organizing these swing components, *The Negotiable Golf Swing* will show you how you can use basic swing components and their permissible permutations to negotiate a better game of golf.

Why negotiate a consistent swing, a better game? Why not simply emulate the model golf swing? Because a negotiable golf swing gets you where you want to go faster and you make that journey with many of the tools that are already in your kit bag. A negotiable golf swing allows for the myriad of individual differences among golfers, and still yields good results. On these pages I will not only identify allowable or negotiable variables—such as swing speed or a floating head, à-la Curtis Strange—but also explain how, after proper assemblage, they produce good results faster than completely tearing apart a swing and rebuilding it.

By understanding how to use basic learning skills, along with the nonnegotiable and negotiable and the link between all of them, a golfer can begin to use his or her own analysis and common sense to negotiate the building of an effective golf swing. To better understand what negotiable means, look no further than the swings of the best players in the world today. Tiger Woods plays with a neutral grip and a model backswing, whereas Jim Furyk plays with a double-overlap grip and a very steep backswing. Fred Couples plays with a strong, closed-faced grip, and Charles Howell with a weaker open-face one. John Daly launches 300-yard drives with an overly long backswing and Allen Doyle successfully plays with a very short backswing. Ernie Els and Retief Goosen swing with a slower tempo than Nick Price and Lanny Wadkins, who swing with a faster one. Many swing concepts focus on trying to convince golfers that they must have perfect form— even a model swing—in order to play better. This is simply not true, and on these pages I will show you why.

How can you build a negotiable golf swing? I'll begin by explaining and showing you how to apply:

1. Basic human learning skills
2. The nonnegotiable, that is, the relationship between the golf club and the golf ball that create the irrefutable laws of the flight of the ball
3. The negotiable, those aforementioned permissible alternatives, such as a strong versus weak grip

In addition, in *The Negotiable Golf Swing*, I will tackle the learning problems that arise from the widespread misinterpretation of all that we read, watch, and eventually take to the practice tee and golf course. Much information or tips that we embrace are myths and "old wives' tales" that, having stubbornly stood the test of time, have become traditional beliefs. I will address these myths and help you separate the wheat from the chaff.

This book doesn't burden the reader with rigid swing models and excessive instruction. Rather, it's an eye-opening tutorial that will empower golfers to create their own personal swings that repeat and get good results. Although my approach will have greater impact among double-digit handicap golfers, *The Negotiable Golf Swing* can help anyone—from beginners to seasoned to single-digit handicap players.

DIRECTION AND DISTANCE: *The Negotiables*

There are many negotiable elements in the golf swing; however, in this book I identify and focus on only the most important ones. The following table lists the negotiable elements in two categories: direction and distance, the two essential factors in all golf shots.

FOR DIRECTION	FOR DISTANCE
Right Elbow	Lateral Backswing Movement
Left Arm at the Top	Amount of Pivot
Backswing Plane	Head and Eyes
Stance	Wrist Set
Grip	Left Arm Bend
Ball Position	Power Source
Posture	Tempo
Alignment	

With a sound understanding of what is nonnegotiable and negotiable in the golf swing, you'll be able to look at your own golf swing and diagnose what you need to work on. You will no longer ride that roller coaster of inconsistency, that pattern of "I got it, I had it, I lost it."

All golfers experience this mysterious, vicious cycle. At times magic comes to us in the form of good-quality consistent golf shots, but then it disappears. You had it last week, but not this week. You had it on the front nine, but not on the back nine. You had it on the last hole, but not on the last shot. What happened? Where did it go? When golfers lose the magic, they struggle to figure out what it was that they had. Finally, they give in and begin again, usually chasing random cures and tips. They don't understand what's absolute or nonnegotiable versus what's negotiable in their swings, which is the key to consistency. They wander down new paths looking for some other swing thought or swing change that they hope will bring back the magic. I have personally experienced this cycle with my own game, only to have it take more wayward bounces than a golf ball rolling across a newly aerated green.

*   *   *

Not long ago, I had a golfer come to me who was very frustrated with his game. At age 50, he had been playing golf for a few years. He was struggling and fed up with being a 25 handicapper. Fairly athletic and relatively strong, he felt he should be much better. The first issue he wanted to address was that he was only hitting his driver about 200 yards, with no control, and the ball was slicing some 20 to 30 yards. He also told me that he didn't have time to practice. His swing was "home grown" with a very unorthodox grip and takeaway.

I started the lesson by explaining to him what the golf club was doing to make the golf ball fly with a big slice. Then, I explained how his grip, a negotiable element, was affecting the movement of the clubface. I suggested we make an adjustment to his grip. Not completely change it to make it conform to the model, but rather modify it, explaining that the grip was negotiable and the modifications would allow for a more effective movement of the golf club, and thus lead to the desired ball flight.

Then, I explained how we needed to change his swing path. He took a few swings to get comfortable with the newly negotiated grip and altered swing path. Within a dozen shots, this golfer was hitting the ball between 260 and 270 yards with a slight draw. He had never seen a ball fly like this, at least not when he was swinging his driver. He stopped and just stared at me in disbelief. He was so excited he was literally shaking. He was amazed that with the same clubhead speed, he was hitting the ball 60 yards farther and straighter just by gripping and routing the club differently.

And the best part of it was that he understood why and that it wasn't a fluke. With his new grip and swing path he soon got down to an 11 handicap. In this case, as it is with most golfers, it was very simple; I just needed to change the golfer's understanding of what the golf club needed to do to improve his ball flight. I can do the same for you, but first let me set a couple of ground rules.

I was recently watching a video in which the famous drummer Neil Peart, was talking about how the phrase "Keep it simple stupid" (K.I.S.S.) is often suggested to drummers. But he felt that K.I.S.S. leads to L.O.V.E.: "Leave out virtually everything." I immediately related this comment to golf. Everyone wants to keep it simple, which is where the birth of many of the tips in golf comes from. It's not that golf instruction has to be complicated and mind-bending, but many times when you try to keep it simple, it inevitably becomes incomplete. Homer Kelly, in his book, *The Golfing Machine*, described it this way:

"Treating a complex subject or action as though it were simple, multiplies its complexity because of the difficulty in systemizing missing and unknown factors or elements. Demanding that golf instruction be kept simple does not make it simple—only incomplete and ineffective. Unless this is recognized, golf remains a vague, frustrating, infuriating form of exertion."

My challenge, then, is to take a relatively complex movement, like the golf swing, and try to simplify it as best I can, yet make it understandable to all readers. That is quite a task. I don't have the luxury (but maybe I will one day) to give you a one-on-one lesson with a dialogue exchange. With that in mind, understand that at times you may miss my point, or you'll say, "What is he talking about?" But I ask that when this does happen, you reread what I've written. If it still doesn't make a connection, leave it for the time being. Think about the idea when you're not reading, maybe when you're driving, or when you are practicing, and then come back to it again.

Another thing that I ask of you is that you do not skip to a section that you think applies to the personal diagnosis you have made with your golf swing. I know that in the past, when I read through the dozens of instruction books, I often skipped to what I thought I needed. It was only years later after rereading the books that I realized how much good-quality information I had passed over. If you choose to skip around and ignore information you don't want to understand or don't think is important, the information you will gather from this book will be incomplete, and your application of this information will be less effective and possibly detrimental to your game. Take your time and contemplate the ideas and observations in this book. Understanding the material in its entirety will be very helpful.

One day a golfer came to my tee for a lesson. He was playing terribly, was distraught, and was seriously considering quitting the game. He was so discouraged that he seriously asked me if I thought it would be a good idea for him to start all over and play left-handed. He then shared an analogy with me. He said, "You don't understand, struggling golfers are desperate. We're like drowning victims. We'll grab on to anything just to stay afloat." His statement was both wrong and right. He was wrong because I did understand the feelings he was describing, both from the perspective of a player and that of a coach. However, I believe his comparison of golfers being akin to drowning victims is very true. In fact, many golfers, in an effort to reach their golfing potential, are waterlogged victims who are barely staying afloat.

Read on and let me throw you a lifeline.

Who Taught You How to Walk?

Who taught you how to walk? Or how to hold a pencil to write? Or how to throw a ball? And did they really teach you? Yes, certain subjects can be taught, such as science and math, but physical motor skills, such as driving a car, jumping a high bar, or riding a bicycle cannot be taught. They must be learned. Much scientific information describes in minute detail the process of how these physical skills, the ones that require motor coordination, are actually learned and performed. But it's not necessary to understand the why and how of physiological processes to understand the learning process. Rather, we can learn much about the learning process by observing humans attempting to perform physical skills. We can especially learn by watching small children, since all the physical skills they learn are new to them.

The process of how we learn a skill is basically the same, regardless of the particular skill. First, we make an attempt to perform the skill. Then, we observe the feedback on our success or failure, and make adjustments based on that feedback. Then, we make another attempt, observe, and adjust. This process continues until we achieve the desired results. As children, when we first learn to walk we lose our balance and fall down, but we keep adjusting to the feedback we experience, steadily improving at the task, until we can walk. When we first learn to throw a ball, we make adjustments based on the weight of the object being thrown and the distance and the direction of the target. If you had a bunch of rocks and were trying to hit a marked target, a bull's eye, with them, you would need to throw the rock an accurate distance and direction. You might miss right and short or left and short or too high or too low. After every throw, you would make adjustments, many of them subconscious, until you arrived at the sequence of physical events that need to take place in order to hit the target with the rock.

We continue to experience this process of learning through feedback from things we do in everyday life. Our mind is an amazing computer, constantly making changes, adjusting and adapting to the environment without our utilizing conscious thought. But feedback is required through our senses of seeing, hearing, or feeling. If we don't have our senses, we have no source of feedback to make performance improvement possible. Imagine standing at the free-throw line on a basketball court. The first source of feedback you would receive is through your vision. You throw up the first shot and miss. Watching the ball miss the basket, for example short and to the right, you observe this result, process it in your brain, and make some adjustments, many of them subconsciously, for the next shot. If you were blindfolded, you could use your hearing as feedback, making adjustments based on what you hear, providing you understood what it sounds like when the ball misses the basket, as opposed to when it goes in. Or if you were blindfolded and someone told you where the ball was missing, you could make adjustments based on that feedback. But if you were blindfolded and wearing earplugs, and I guided you to the foul line and gave you some balls, it would be impossible for you to accurately perform the skill of making baskets from the foul line. Without some source of feedback, we cannot perform or improve our skills.

Let's practice a simple physical task while reading this book. I've already expressed that my other passion, besides golf, is playing the drums. It's a skill that requires a great deal of coordination, sometimes necessitating all four limbs to do different things at the same time. I've created an exercise based on learning a drum pattern. You can do this exercise as you read this book. Everyone has tapped his or her hands or fingers on a table at one time or another, or has played "air drums" during a favorite song. In this exercise, we start with a basic drum pattern—in drumming it's called a rudiment. You can learn to do it by tapping with your pointer fingers on this book, or using your hands on your thighs. The letters R and L represent a note or tap of the hand or finger you will use, with R meaning right hand

and L meaning left hand. I've spaced each grouping of the four notes apart to make it easier, but it is continuous with no breaks or rests in the pattern. After the first two groups, the line repeats itself. The rudiment is called a paradiddle because the word and the four syllables it contains help you verbalize the pattern as you play it.

The pattern looks like this:

(keep repeating)

Start out slowly and build up the speed, making the taps as evenly spaced as possible. Do this for about 20 or 30 seconds. Try to smoothly build up the speed of the pattern as fast as you can. At some point, the evenness of the sounds is lost. When this happens, slow down until the notes sound more evenly spaced and then try to build up speed again. At this stage of your new drumming skills, this is the fastest point where you can make the motion and still get the desired result of evenness and continuity of the sound of the pattern. This exercise pattern is quite simple, but not necessarily easy since it is a new skill for you. Don't feel bad if you struggle; there are some drummers who can do this faster with their feet then I can with my hands.

Through this exercise, what we can observe is that your basic feedback source is sound, which you are obtaining through your hearing, with another source being the feel in your fingers or hands. You probably are not thinking of it, but your mind figures out how hard and fast for your fingers to move to create an even sound between each note. Your mind makes adjustments when receiving this feedback and tells your body what adjustments to make. The two important things to recognize about this exercise are that you are learning and adjusting through feedback and that you learn the basic skill of performing these patterns slowly before being able to do it efficiently at faster speeds.

Through the observations we have made we can create a basic learning model that would look like this:

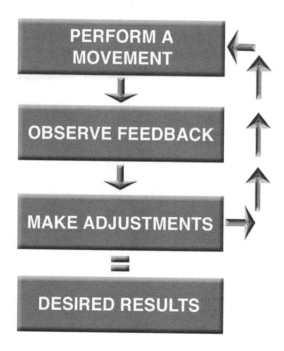

PERFORM A MOVEMENT

↓

OBSERVE FEEDBACK

↓

MAKE ADJUSTMENTS

=

DESIRED RESULTS

Let's discuss this further by taking a look at how you might go about teaching someone else a physical skill that requires motor coordination. Say you're going to teach someone who hasn't driven before how to drive a car. You drive this person to a vacant parking lot, turn the car off, and switch seats. Now, how are you going to teach this person to drive? When I think about this question, I think I would tell the person to put the key in the ignition and turn the key to the right. When the car starts, I would tell the person to stop turning the key. Then, I would point to the gas and brake pedals and explain that pushing the gas pedal causes the car to accelerate, and pushing the brake pedal causes the car to slow down or come to a complete stop. Then, I would say that the steering wheel controls the direction of the car, and I would point out the location of the mirrors and indicate what letters on the gear shift are for park, neutral, and drive. Now, if I got out of the car, could this person learn to drive without any other teaching? Isn't this more than enough information? What do you think? What more would you have told him or her? Many of you probably would have said at least what I said to the person learning, and many would have given further instructions, such as, "Put your hands at the 10:00 and 2:00 positions and use only one foot when working the pedals." Some of you would add even more information. But is all of that information really contributing to how the person is learning the skill? Aren't they just suggestions? Let me explain.

When the person sat down in the seat, did you need to indicate where and how to sit? Did you tell how to hold the key when placing it in the ignition, and how hard to turn the key? Did you indicate how to move his or her legs and ankles to operate the pedals? Did you tell how to move his or her hands, arms, and elbows to get the steering wheel to function correctly? If you think about it, the person would be able to learn to drive the car with the little information that I suggested. The person would learn how far to turn the key and when to release it, how much pressure each pedal needs to speed up or slow down, and how much to turn the wheel this way or that way to make the car go in this or that direction. Through trial and error, the person would learn the fundamental skill of driving a car.

I'd offer other suggestions to the new driver, such as looking in the rearview mirror every so often, checking the side mirrors, looking before changing lanes, and so on. But these would be to help the person drive safely. The fundamental skill of driving the car would be learned by the driver through experience.

Humans are problem-solvers by nature and use the experience of self-discovery to learn physical skills. The other day, I was sitting on my couch and my 5-year-old son wanted to throw a little foam ball to me. He was about 10 feet away from me. Now, my son mostly plays with his trucks and other toys. At this point, he hadn't shown any interest in sports and had no experience throwing a ball. I said to myself this was going to be a disaster, with the possibility of the ball going every which way. He threw the ball to me in an overhand style and, to my surprise, it got pretty close to me. As he continued throwing the ball to me, his accuracy improved. Then, for some reason, he began to throw the ball with a sidearm and underhand style. The ball was going all over the room. I became intrigued observing him throw the ball. Because his best success was coming from the overhand method, I encouraged him to keep doing it that way. When he did one of the other methods, I reinforced the idea of throwing overhand. After about 15 minutes, I was shocked at how accurately he was throwing the ball to me. But during this process, I wasn't instructing him on how to use his elbow or when to release the ball from his hand. He was just throwing the ball, learning from the visual feedback, and letting his subconscious calculate the adjustments. For a child who really had no experience throwing objects to a target, he did amazingly well. Maybe he's got some potential, but, of course, since then he's gone back to his computer games and other toys and hasn't asked to play catch.

Other observations are important about the learning process. We don't teach children how to walk by talking about the hip, knee, and ankle movement in walking, or how the heel must make contact with the ground before the toes. Generally speaking, we learn by doing small things before big things; we take little steps before taking big steps. We also learn movements slowly, before learning to do them at a faster pace. We learn to walk before we learn to run. In essence, we learn through self-discovery and the understanding of the environment in which we learn. I'll also bet that when cavemen learned to throw a spear, someone wasn't around communicating the actual individual movements needed to throw the spear. I'll also venture to guess that there wasn't a detailed manual carved on the inside of the wall of their cave. Learning a physical skill needs to be learned through self-discovery, a process of adjusting to feedback and experimenting through trial and error until the desired results are achieved.

While learning through self-discovery, though, one has to be careful about using too much conscious thought to achieve good performance. Recently I went to Chuck E Cheese, an indoor amusement place that has games and rides for small children. While my wife was chasing my son around the place, I grabbed some tokens and headed over to the basketball game. It's the game with small basketballs and a basket. The game is caged in, close to you and probably only about six feet high. You insert the token, the machine releases a few balls, and you keep shooting for 30 seconds and see how many baskets you can make in that allotted time. When I first started, I was terrible. I missed left, right, short, and long. After the first game, I would rate my performance as horrific. Then, I started thinking hard about how I was using my arm and wrist and how I was releasing the ball from my finger tips. My results were no better; at times they were worse. But because the competitive side of me would not allow my ego to settle for this level of performance, I continued to drop tokens into the machine, relaxed a little more, and focused on the target, allowing my subconscious to make the necessary adjustments based on the feedback I was observing and feeling. I steadily improved and continued to drop tokens into the machine until I performed at a level that was satisfactory to my ego.

When an athlete misses an important shot during a crucial time, this is sometimes referred to as "choking," meaning that a player messed up because of the pressure. But failing to perform is often caused by the conscious mind trying to control the individual's physical movements, which in turn interferes with the subconscious mind. One of the interesting things I observed while playing that basketball game is that when I consciously tried to adjust things, my performance did not improve and at times it actually got worse. Most performance coaches would agree that conscious thought interferes with subconscious thought, or as Homer Kelly said, "Conscious thought annoys subconscious thought." When you perform physical skills, conscious thought can have an adverse effect on performance. I remember when I was a kid playing Little League baseball as the pitcher on the team. From time to time, I would struggle with my control and had trouble throwing strikes. As the pressure to throw more accurately increased, my pitching became wilder. I remember my father calling out to me from the sidelines, "Stop steering the ball, and just let it go." Basically, he was telling me to stop my conscious thinking, look at the target, and let my subconscious—the key to unlocking my skills—do the work.

Conscious thought is not the only thing that affects performance. I suffer from acrophobia, a fear of heights. I experience this phobia even when I watch movies where someone is hanging from a building or a cliff. My hands start to sweat and my heart rate becomes elevated. When I was a young child, my mother tells me that when we drove over the Throgs Neck Bridge, which was every Sunday on our way to visit my grandmother, I would crouch down on the floor of the back seat of the car. Today, when I drive over a bridge, my hands sweat and my grip tightens on the steering wheel to the point that it would take the strength of several Clydesdale horses to pull my hands off the wheel. Like everybody else, I consider myself a fairly good driver, one who really enjoys driving sports cars. But when making a simple lane change on a bridge, I become very conscious of my movements with the steering wheel and the pressure I apply to the brakes. If I were driving on an obstacle course and you asked me to perform the skill of weaving around and between a row of cones at a relatively fast speed, I'm confident I could handle that task. But on a bridge, I would freeze under the same conditions. I could do the cone slalom on the bridge, but the car would probably only be moving about three miles per hour. Anxiety can impact performance.

In any physical skill that requires motor coordination, the skills can't be taught. Trying to learn them piece by piece, like assembling a bicycle, is ineffective. Conscious thought and anxiety play a role in performance, degenerating it more times than not. This is not to say that some conscious thought and awareness are not necessary to learn an activity or improve at it. However, the amount of conscious thought we process during performance is what is important. Our ability to do less conscious thinking when performing can lead to better performance. All these aspects of the learning process apply to learning an effective golf swing.

CHAPTER 2

The Learning Model and Golfers

We've seen in the learning model a sequence of events that takes place when performing any physical skill. No doubt golf is a physical skill that requires motor coordination. You use your body to hold and swing the golf club, and with that club, you strike a golf ball with the goal of getting the ball to a specific target. Like the other physical skills that we've talked about, golf cannot be taught. It must be learned. Someone can give you suggestions about what to do to play golf well, but like learning to drive a car or throw a ball, you have to learn yourself what to do.

Let's plug a golf shot and learning golf into our learning model. With some modification and an addition, the model for learning looks like the diagram at right.

If we use the learning model for physical skills, we should be able to use it for playing golf. Right? We should be able to use the model for any type of golf shot from a putt to a drive. Right? However, most golfers believe they are using the

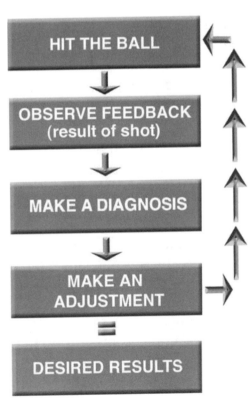

HIT THE BALL

OBSERVE FEEDBACK
(result of shot)

MAKE A DIAGNOSIS

MAKE AN
ADJUSTMENT

=

DESIRED RESULTS

above formula, but listen to most of them and you'll hear that they aren't improving their game, no matter how much they make swing changes. As mentioned earlier, occasionally golfers find a swing thought that seems to work well, but the positive results are fleeting. Why aren't they using the learning model effectively?

There are several reasons that explain why the learning model breaks down with golfers. Many times a golfer will grab onto a swing thought and hold on to it for dear life even though it is a hindrance to an effective golf swing. For instance, during a lesson a golfer once told me that he was working on something specific: keeping his head down throughout his swing. I resisted the urge to comment on this and had him hit a few shots. During the first few swings, I said nothing, but captured every swing on my video system. Struggling, the golfer hit a few poor shots, all the while clearly keeping his head down, with his eyes glued to the ground, to the point where I wasn't sure if he could see where the ball was going. After hitting a few poor shots, he finally connected and hit a shot fairly solid and straight. He then turned to me and said, "You see. I kept my head down on that one." I then played back the video of the shot he hit well. He could clearly see that he kept his head down well past impact. He said that as long as he could do that, he could hit the ball well. Then, I showed him the other swings when he hit the ball poorly. Basically, the swings all looked the same, with him clearly performing the objective of keeping his head down. He looked at me with that puzzled look all golfers have in their expression toolbox. The fact of the matter was that his swing key, the position of his head, had nothing to do with the success of the shot. He hit one good shot in spite of what he thought he was working on. This is an example of the conscious mind working with an ineffective swing thought and the subconscious part of the mind working toward trying to strike the ball effectively. Sometimes the subconscious mind achieves its goal through making minute adjustments and compensations, despite the thoughts of the conscious mind.

Sometimes I work with a golfer who is suffering from the shanks, the dreaded shot that strikes the hosel of the club and shoots off to the right at about a forty-five degree angle. It's an unplayable shot, and I've witnessed golfers walk off the course in the middle of a round

The shank shot causes the ball to fly low and sharply to the right.

because of it. What's interesting is that when most golfers first experience this shot, they don't believe the ball is striking the hosel. In fact, many think that it's going off the other end, the toe of the club, causing the ball to go sharply to the right. How do they offset this? They consciously move closer to the ball in an effort to make sure the clubhead strikes the ball closer to the center of the clubface. But, of course, this just makes the problem worse. This is an example of how learning golf can be counterintuitive, leading us to believe one thing is happening when in reality it is the exact opposite. I've experienced the same thing many times with my own game. After I changed from hitting a fade, and started to draw the ball, sometimes I would miss left, sometimes really far to the left. My conscious mind would say that I must be swinging the club to the left, on an outside-in clubhead path. I would swing more inside out to prevent the ball from going left. But unbeknownst to me at the time, it was my inside-out swing path that was causing the left shot. The more I hit it to the left, the more inside out I swung and the farther to the left the ball went. I was being fouled by the feedback that I thought I was observing. It was a frustrating, vicious circle that went on for some time.

Another problem that interferes with the effectiveness of the learning model for golfers is the abundance of information with which golfers are being bombarded. I went to Amazon.com and searched the words "golf instruction." The search returned a number of results that exceeded one thousand books and DVDs. In addition, golfers have access to monthly golf magazines and the Golf Channel. All of the professional tournaments are now broadcast, including examples of tour players' swings with slow motion pictures and commentary offered to viewers. However, much of the information that is available to golfers is conflicting in theory. Or it is misunderstood, misapplied, incomplete, or oversimplified. Some of the information is completely inaccurate, but appears logical and convincing with a forced perspective. In my early teaching years, I took ideas that appeared very logical and convinced both myself and my students of the relevancy and importance of certain concepts. I spent years experimenting, jumping from theory to theory, concept to concept, in an effort to find the magic that would take my game to new levels. Now, before the entire golfing community seeks me out for a lynching, I'm not suggesting that all of the information out there is worthless. On the contrary, an abundance of it offers very sound concepts. However, it is difficult to sort through all of the available information in all of its forms. The abundance of information provides hundreds of suggestions and secrets that can temporarily improve one's golf game. I find that most golfers randomly choose swing thoughts and make changes with the hope that improvement will take place. This method is many times nothing more than a golfer taking a stab in the dark, an effort to catch lightning in a bottle, so to speak. Working on and changing the position of your elbow at the top just because you heard an expert state the importance of it does not necessarily lead to improvement. Many times when a golfer changes something, it impacts and changes something else. For example, if you change your backswing, it may change the position of your arms at the top, which in turn may change your downswing. Or sometimes, two things need to be changed together for improvement to take place. But randomly choosing quick tips and fixes and trying to employ them is not going to help a golfer improve.

Do You Know Where Your Golf Swing Is?

Even when armed with all of the correct information, golfers still face another challenge with the learning model. That challenge is that golfers don't understand the state of their present swing. If you ask many golfers about their swing, they'll describe it in detail like they were holding it in front of them in their hands; but to the contrary, I witness the following occurrence all the time. I'll videotape a golfer's swing and before I comment on it, I have him or her watch

Within the illustration: "FEEL TAKEAWAY", "REAL TAKEAWAY", 12"

Reality and what a golfer feels is happening are usually two very different things.

it in real-time speed in a mode that repeats the swing over and over. Upon seeing the swing for the first time, the golfer is surprised that it doesn't look like how it felt and that it includes things he or she never imagined he or she was doing.

I remember my first video lesson very clearly. It was the early '90s and a couple of members took me on a golfing trip to Cobblestone

Country Club in Stuart, Florida. While there, I took a video lesson from Dr. Jim Suttie, a well-known instructor and co-author of the book, *The Laws of the Golf Swing*. I can still vividly recall watching the video playback with Suttie, and the disbelief at what I was seeing. The video looked nothing like what I felt I was doing. This disbelief is one of the major obstacles that golfers face; they believe they are doing something when in fact they are not, or they are doing the exact opposite.

Therefore, many times our feelings and perceptions get in the way of our understanding and ability to diagnose a problem and incorporate new changes. I've had golfers insist that they are "sliding ahead," moving past the ball at impact, as opposed to staying back and behind it. But when I show them that this is not the case, they are usually bewildered. They can't see themselves swing the club. They can only feel what they are doing, and they tend to believe what they feel. A golfer may be working on shortening his backswing to gain more control. When making the change, he feels like he is moving the club back a foot less than normal. But the reality is that it's only a couple of inches. A video reveals the differences between what an individual experiences internally and what is actually happening. I remember when I worked on shortening my golf swing in an attempt to gain some control. It wasn't a really long swing, but I thought if I shortened it that it would become more repeatable. I was only shortening my swing about six inches, but I swear that when I was doing it, it felt as if I were taking the club back only to about waist-high. I would play back the video and I couldn't believe the difference between what I felt I was doing and what I was actually doing.

These several reasons interfere and prevent golfers from utilizing their inherent learning skills; they are not using the learning model to effectively improve their golf swing. But they can, and I am going to show you how.

First, golfers need to understand the importance of feedback in the learning process. It is essential to achieving our goals. Without it, we can't properly monitor our progress and make the necessary adjustments to achieve our goals. Imagine going to the range and hitting balls into total darkness. All you see is the ball on the ground in front of you. After you hit the ball, it goes into the darkness. How could you possibly improve? You could make observations about how it felt to hit the ball, but none about where the ball went.

In golf, our primary source of feedback in the learning model is the flight of the ball or the path the ball takes after it comes off the clubface, whether it's a slice, a hook, a straight shot, high, low, a chip, or a putt. It stands to reason then that golfers need to understand this relationship between the club and the ball, a relationship termed "ball flight." Most golfers think they understand ball flight, but they don't. I know this from experience, both as a golfer and as a teacher. When I'm working with golfers, in the very beginning of the lesson, I'll ask what the problem is and they'll tell me how the ball is slicing or hooking, or that they're topping it, or whatever other unacceptable ball flight they are experiencing. Sometimes the first question I ask them is "What is the golf club doing to produce that result?" Most golfers look at me with a quizzical expression and shrug their shoulders. They just don't know. Golfers understand general things like "I slice the ball because I'm cutting across it" or "to hit a hook, I need to swing from inside out." But do you know what the clubface should look like at impact? Do you know why your short irons go straighter than your long irons? Do you know that if you curve the ball, in either direction, that you need to aim at thirteen different targets to be accurate? If you don't know the answers to these questions, then you really don't understand ball flight. Since golfers don't understand the ball's relationship with the club, the nonnegotiable laws of ball flight, success utilizing this model is doomed from the start.

Another very important aspect of learning and improving your game is to understand the golf swing. But this knowledge and understanding must be of what a functional and effective golf swing is. Not necessarily the perfect model swing, the stuff you mostly hear and read about, but rather what makes a swing functional, what is negotiable and nonnegotiable in the golf swing. Golfers are working without this knowledge. While working with golfers, I'll show them a picture of a sound functional golf swing, usually that of a tour player, and put it up against their swing. I'll ask them what they think is going on, the difference between the two. Despite seeing it, their observations are usually a reflection of the preconceived notion of what they think they are doing wrong. They'll make observations and comment on what the professional player is doing with his knees, hips, or head. Yet, none of these things are areas they need to focus on. Even if you gave most golfers a video of their swing and let them work on it by themselves, they probably still wouldn't improve because they don't understand what they are looking at and what to look for. Many are busy trying to model the perfect swing, a model swing that they're not capable of producing for various reasons. In fact, many times, because of this lack of knowledge, I see golfers change things for the worse. I can't even tell you the number of times that I changed something in my golf swing, which was fundamentally sound, for the worse, because I was working on something else, ideas that were irrelevant to why I was struggling at the time.

To diagnose and make changes to improve their golf swing, golfers need to understand the components, or what I like to refer to as elements, of the golf swing. These elements can be broken down into two types: pre-swing and in-swing. Examples of pre-swing elements are anything that takes place before the swing is in motion, such as posture, grip, and stance. In-swing elements can be anything that takes place during the swing, such as when and how the wrists, arms, legs, shoulders, or just about any body part you can think of, moves during the swing. Ideally, after a golfer observes the ball's flight, an element can be adjusted that will influence the club, which in turn will influence the ball's flight.

Now, we can modify our golf learning model to look like the diagram on page 39.

Again, this model can be applied to any part of the game, from putting to the full swing. Improvement for many golfers is not only about understanding the relationship between the club and the ball, the pre-swing and in-swing elements, and the impact they have on the movement of the golf club. The diagnosis process must start with observing the ball flight and what the club did to create that ball flight. Then, when needed, the appropriate element can be focused on and modified. This is where the challenge of diagnosis exists. If the elements and their impact are not fully understood, diagnosing and changing elements can be a futile, frustrating, and sometimes complete waste of time and effort.

It's also very helpful, if not imperative, to understand the human

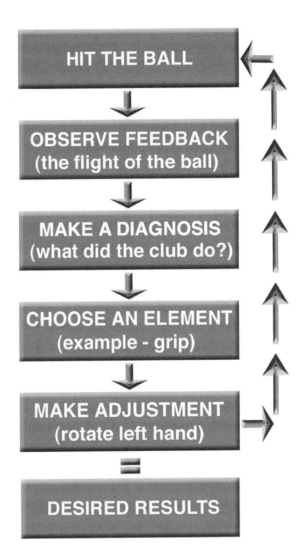

body and its influence on the elements. The popularity of golf fitness is growing with good reason. The golf swing is an athletic movement that requires flexibility, strength, and balance, and it's very important for golfers to understand their own physical attributes and limitations. There is now an abundance of information on this topic in books and DVDs, as well as physical fitness programs specifically designed for golfers being offered at fitness clubs and physical therapy facilities throughout the country. I believe it is in the best interest of your game to explore this area and, with the permission of your doctor, embark on a program.

As you can see, golfers are faced with many challenges when working toward learning and improving. The model, for any physical activity or task, works for all individuals. It's not that the model needs to be learned by golfers, because all humans instinctively know how to use it. But rather two things must take place. The first is that everything that is running interference with the model needs to be eliminated. The second is that everything within the model needs to be understood.

3

Form, Function, and the Negotiable Elements of Style

Golfers talk much about the form of the swing and the techniques to produce effective swings and better, more predictable results. Look at this photo below of me hitting a ball off a tee that's used by young kids playing "tee ball" (the arrow represents the direction of center field).

Which way is the ball going to go, to the left or to the right? It's pretty obvious that the ball will go to the right. If instead I wanted to hit the ball straight to center field, what would I need to do? If you said to make sure that at impact the bat is facing more toward center field, as opposed to right field, you would be correct. But if I hit a golf ball to the right and take a picture of my golf swing at impact, chances are most golfers, and some experts, would focus on some body part--such as the head, hips, or elbow—being out of position. A few years ago, I would have been included in this group. In fact, focus-

ing on body position, or form, was the only way that I worked on my own game, as well as the method I employed when helping other golfers work on their swings. Of course, there has been some success with this methodology, but I have found that this is not the most effective way for golfers to improve their golf swing.

The word form is probably best defined as the "golf swing model," the one that you see in magazines, books, and on television. It's the perfect golf swing, one with all the elements in the perfect place and in the correct sequence. It's the swing that I studied, like so many golfers, in an effort to emulate every part and position. Many instructors and golfers use the word efficient as a term to describe a swing that is close to the model. It brings with it the connotation of a swing without wasted motion. But the most important thing to understand when building a better swing is how to get the club to function in a way that produces the desirable ball flight, whether it's to curve the ball in any direction, high or low, straight, to the right, or to the left. I consider a swing effective, regardless of the form being used, when it gets the club to function in a way that consistently produces the desired results. Golfers need to focus on making their swings more effective.

The golf community is so focused on form and the perfect golf swing that it's no surprise that the bulk of tips and theories are about form. We have become obsessed with the movement of the body, as opposed to the movement of the golf club. Several years ago, I was driving in a car with my father on the way to a father/son tournament. As I mentioned earlier, my dad was a real student of the game. While driving to the tournament, we listened to a tape of someone, I believe a sports psychologist, discussing the golf swing. I remember the person asking the question, "Are you looking for good form or good function?" Interestingly, back then I didn't even think about form, much less study the golf swing. I just thought about making the ball go straight, and thus had a relatively unorthodox swing. But based on his in-depth studying, my dad did focus on form. I asked him which one he wanted: good form or good function. He replied, "Both." Today, my response to his answer would be that if we get the club to function effectively, many times the form will also improve. Hence, in many ways form can follow function. Nowadays, many instructors teach and golfers learn the opposite way, by trying to learn form first, with the intention of function following. Because we don't learn other things this way, I consider this a backward method of learning.

Understand that you do not need to have perfect form in order to get the club to function effectively. This is not to say that focusing on the body is a poor or ineffective way to think; it just depends on what the golfer is thinking about. Over the years I've focused on my toes, knees, thighs, hamstrings, hips, buttocks, rib cage, chest, elbows, eyes, neck, shoulders, wrists, fingers, elbows, and forearms. Unfortunately, many times this was done randomly as a result of studying swing sequences or written material that focused on swinging like the "model," and most of the time was ineffective. This is how most golfers choose to change elements: on a random basis with a focus on the model swing. The difference for me now is that when I focus on changing a particular movement with my body, I understand how the change affects the movement of the golf club and whether or not the change is negotiable. For instance, a particular element, such as the grip, should only be addressed if it is negatively affecting the movement of the golf club.

Many golfers will point to tour players to illustrate how all their golf swings look the same and are perfect model swings. Not true. Some stand with an open stance, some take the club above the plane during the takeaway, some move their heads back more than others on the backswing, and so on. Fred Couples, Lee Trevino, and Jim Furyk, along with many others, have unorthodox swings. Jack Nicklaus played with a "flying elbow," and he did okay, didn't he? If you look closely and understand what you're looking at, you'll see many more of the differences among the swings of the best players in the world than you may have originally thought existed. Many will credit the success of some tour players to the fact that they do have a swing that closely resembles the model. This may be a valid point; however, I believe there have been players we'll never hear about, or others who were on their way to success but fell off the radar screen, all because they were trying so hard to conform to the model and create a swing with perfect form, as opposed to sticking with their own unique way of swinging the golf club. Successful players with less

Jack Nicklaus and his flying elbow.

than orthodox swings are usually credited with resources, such as an amazing natural ability and the time to hit thousands of golf balls to groove that unusual movement. But if they have so much talent and time to hit balls, which they do, why don't they change to the model if it is a much better way of swinging the golf club? The answer is that they found the best way to swing the club is their own individual way.

If you are trying to build a swing with perfect form, you have to ask yourself some questions. Do you possess the strength, flexibility, and coordination to build this type of swing, and if so, do you have the time and the resources to build it? Most golfers don't. As I mentioned earlier, the golf swing requires a combination of balance, strength, and flexibility. If your body has weaknesses and limitations, you may not be able to perform many of the movements you are trying to execute. In fact, if you are not aware of these limitations and are attempting to execute movements that you cannot physically perform, it's very likely you'll have more struggles with your swing, with the possibility of making it worse. Many of these struggles are caused by golfers trying to do things that their bodies are incapable of doing. I remember taking lessons on two different occasions with two different instructors, both well respected nationally. Both instructors were "hands on" and were physically trying to put me into the model positions they were suggesting. The problem was that in both cases my limited flexibility would not allow me to get into these positions, and when I did, it was actually painful. I understood why they wanted me to be in these positions, but unless I was able to improve my flexibility, there was no way I could perform those movements. The mind will fight the body when trying to perform movements that cause physical discomfort.

The important thing to understand is that the swing that will work for you can be very unique. In a way, it can be like a fingerprint. But the first thing you need to understand is what is negotiable and what is nonnegotiable in the golf swing. In the next chapter, I'll talk about the laws of ball flight and the influence of the golf club's movement on the ball flight. These laws are nonnegotiable and are governed by physics, the laws of the physical world. However, the things that you do in the swing to move the golf club, the elements of the swing, are negotiable. For example, no one grip exists for every player. You don't

PGA Tour player Jim Furyk has an unorthodox yet very effective swing.

need to take the club back on a certain path to make an effective swing. Your elbow can be in an unorthodox position at the top and still make an effective downswing. However, to allow for these unique and individual elements, you need to understand how they impact the movement of the golf club, which in turn affects the flight of the golf ball. Your goal should not be to make a perfect swing, but rather to find a combination of elements that are compatible for you and that you can physically perform to produce a predictable ball flight.

I remember a few years ago Jim Furyk, who has one of the most unique swings on tour, was working on trying to change his backswing and the position of his arms to something that closer resembled the model. I wasn't personally observing these changes; I just happened to be watching a tour event when Furyk was on the range and the commentators were talking about how he was changing this and that to be more consistent. You could see what he was working on, including some drastic changes. I don't know what exactly transpired, but a few months later I saw him swinging the way he did before trying to make those changes, the same swing that won him tournaments, one being a major championship. My guess is that he came to the conclusion that he had his own unique swing and it's what he needed to stick with to be successful and win golf tournaments.

Individuality in style is something that exists in many sports and physical activities. Look at baseball players. They don't all look the same when they are at the plate getting ready to swing at a 90 mph fastball. I personally experienced developing my own style with drumming. In the Preface, I talked about taking drumming lessons with Dom Famularo. It was no surprise that the first things we worked on were my grip and my posture, important elements in drumming as well as in golf. After Dom showed me the correct technique, I worked on it for hours. But over time, what happened was that I started

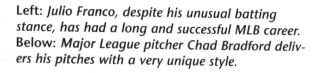

Left: *Julio Franco, despite his unusual batting stance, has had a long and successful MLB career.* Below: *Major League pitcher Chad Bradford delivers his pitches with a very unique style.*

to modify this model grip. I haven't gone back to Dom since, but I always had a fear of how he would respond to the individual adjustments I made to my grip. I assumed that even though my skills were improving, what I was doing was wrong because the style I had developed didn't conform to the model grip. Recently, I was reading a drum magazine that had interviews with some of the most famous drummers in the world being asked questions about their grips. Many of them were using the same modifications that I had naturally adopted in my grip technique. The modifications were somewhat unorthodox, according to the model, but still very effective. It's amazing how much my playing improved by understanding and changing the fundamental elements of my grip and posture, and their impact on the function of the movement of a drumstick. When I think about it, I believe Dom would be just fine with my changes.

Having a unique golf swing is something that should be embraced, not necessarily changed. When golfers come to me with an element, a particular movement, in their swing that is somewhat unusual but I don't believe needs to be changed, I encourage them to see it as something unique and to show others how well they can play with it, as opposed to being self-conscious about it. When I work with golfers I don't address anything that is unorthodox unless I see that the particular element is causing the player difficulties in getting the club to function effectively. And even then, I only adjust it the amount it needs to be changed. For example, let's say a player is taking the club on a very inside path on the backswing, causing the player difficulty in getting the club on an effective path on the downswing. I don't automatically go right to the golf swing model and try to build the perfect model backswing. I may use the concept as a guideline, but if a few inches of change can make the difference, why do I need to get the player to go farther than that? In a sense, I use a minimalist approach.

There are some golfers I work with who have very unique and unorthodox elements in their golf swings. About a year ago, I had a golfer come to me and ask if a change he made was acceptable. He stood far enough away from the ball so that when he soled his club, the clubhead was several inches away from the ball. He looked like he was going to take a practice swing. Then, he took a swing from this position and hit the ball. I filmed the swing and looked at it. He hit a few more shots, shots that he was pleased with and that were fairly consistent. If I had seen this several years ago, I would have jumped in and said it was wrong and tried to justify my reasoning. But after watching him hit a few shots, I could see that the club was functioning fairly well and that he was satisfied with the ball flight. How could I argue with that? I sent him away with an approval and he's still playing with that unorthodox setup. I have another student who has a very unusual grip. When he's struggling, the grip is the first thing other golfers notice. But the fact of the matter is that I don't change his grip because it still allows the club to function in a manner that is effective. Several golfers I work with have relatively long backswings, similar to tour players John Daly and Carlos Franco, with the club well past parallel at the top of the backswing. But once again, if they can still get the club to function and it's not an element that's preventing it from happening, I consider it negotiable and I don't touch it.

Recently *Golf Magazine* published a feature article about the next golf superstar, a boy from Scotland named Reece Murphy. Some believe he has more talent at his age than did Tiger Woods or Michelle Wie. He's 6 years old, stands 4'2", and weighs 44 pounds; at age 3 he tied Tiger's record lowest nine-hole score at the same age. He drives the ball about 145 yards, has a great short game, and routinely shoots in the mid-forties for nine holes. Reece has an unconventional swing, including a very unorthodox grip: a left-hand low or what is sometimes called a cross-handed grip, basically holding the club like a left-hander, but playing right-handed. Curious about Reece's use of

Young Reece Murphy has found his own way of swinging the club effectively.

the grip and whether others were trying to change it, I contacted his father, Steven, by e-mail and asked him about it. He told me a story that summed it all up. Reece was practicing one day at a prestigious golf course when one of the young pros came over and started watching Reece hit some balls. After watching Reece hit one good shot after another, the pro stepped in, told him he was doing it wrong, and physically changed his grip to a conventional one. Reece continued to hit one good shot after another with the new grip as the pro looked on, smiled, and commented on how this was the way Reece needed to do it. Reece then turned to him, said "I like my grip better," and went on to hit good shots with his preferred grip. The pro started to tell him that he would have to change to be a good player, and before he could finish his sentence, Reece thanked him and told him he would change his grip if and when he wanted to. The pro walked away. Reece's father told me that it's his belief that if it works for Reece, then why should they change it? I agree. Apparently Reece, while unconventional, has found his own way to get the club to function effectively.

Experimenting with different elements as an individual allows a golfer freedom and an environment to find what works for him or her, and allows for the process of learning through self-discovery to take place. The imperative things are to gain a better understanding of your use of the elements and how they affect the movement of the golf club. Once you understand these things, you can start building your own swing. And as long as your swing elements don't cause a violation to the nonnegotiable laws of the physical world, your golf swing can be unique and efficient as well as functional and effective.

CHAPTER 4

Factors that Affect Ball Flight Patterns

We live in a physical world, one that is governed by the laws of physics. These physical laws allow us to predict things that will happen. They are absolutes and are nonnegotiable. Something happens, and then something else happens as a result of it. If you drop a ball from a particular height onto a hard surface, it will bounce back up a certain height. If you hammer a nail with a certain amount of force, the nail will be driven into the surface a certain depth. All causes, when exactly reproduced, will produce identical effects. This is referred to as cause and effect. In golf, a club is used to strike a ball. The cause, the club, has an effect on the flight of the ball. Simply put, golf is nothing more than a stick-and-ball game; we use a stick to hit the ball. And we need to make the ball do two things: go a distance in a certain direction. The cause and effect is an irrefutable relationship between the golf club and the golf ball. The collision between the club and ball, if exactly repeated either positively or negatively, will produce the same results every time.

This cause and effect relationship needs to be understood because it is the primary source of our feedback in golf, and hence a necessary ingredient in the learning model. I vividly remember playing a casual round where one of the golfers hit a really unusual-looking poor tee shot that went very low and to the right. The golfer turned around and looked at me bewildered and said "How did that happen?" That moment really drove home the fact that most golfers, and in this instance the golfer was a single-digit handicap player, just don't understand the cause and effect between the club and the ball. A golfer should be able to watch the ball knowing what the club did to produce that result.

If you were stranded on a desert island and had only a set of clubs and a bunch of balls, the only feedback you would have would be ball flight. No mirrors, no video, no instructor, and no second set of eyes. However, without knowledge of cause and effect, most golfers would take a long time, if ever, to figure out how the relationship between the club and ball works because it can be very confusing and counterintuitive. I love to hear golfers say "let the club do the work." This commonly heard phrase sounds really good and very simple—if you understand how the club works. For most golfers this is really an empty concept that is much too vague. There's certainly truth in the statement; however, in order to let the club do the work, you need to understand how the club is designed to function and how it affects the flight of a golf ball.

In golf, there is what is referred to as the laws that determine ball flight. These laws are irrefutable for all golfers and for all golf shots. Five major laws affect the flight of a golf ball, each of them having a primary influence on either distance or direction, with some secondary influence on the other. The laws are speed, centeredness of contact, path, face angle, and angle of approach.

1. Speed. How fast the club moves (speed) determines how far the ball will go. The faster the club is moving, the more force is transferred to the golf ball, resulting in increased distance. The primary effect of speed is distance, with a secondary effect on direction. Each club in the bag is a different length. The significance of this difference is that longer clubs move faster than shorter clubs. If you gripped a driver and a pitching wedge at the same time and swung them together, your body, arms, and hands would be moving at a certain speed, and both clubheads would be traveling at the same rate of rotation, but the clubhead of the driver would be moving faster than the clubhead of the wedge because it has a bigger arc and therefore is traveling a farther distance. For example, imagine you are in the sky looking down at a merry-go-round and there are three circles of horses. The horses on the inside circle are a relatively short distance from the center of the merry-go-round. That distance represents a short iron. The

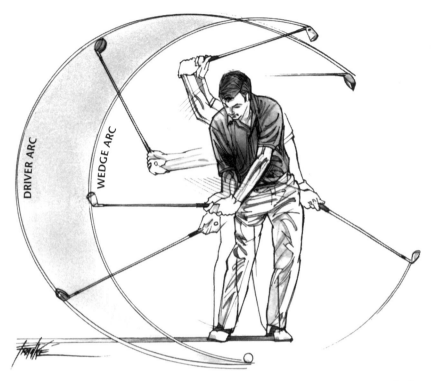

Even though the body, arms, and hands are moving at the same speed, the clubhead of the driver moves faster than the clubhead of the wedge because it has a bigger arc.

horses on the outside circle are a farther distance away from the center, and that distance represents the driver. When the merry-go-round is spinning, the horses on the inside are rotating at the same rate as those on the outside, but the horses on the outside are moving on a bigger circle, or arc, thereby traveling a longer distance, which means they are moving faster than the horses on the inside. This also explains the reason why many golfers, when stuck between say a five or six iron, grip down on the five iron so that they can hit it a little shorter distance; the shorter length creates a smaller arc and reduces the speed of the clubhead.

2. *Centeredness of Contact.* Centeredness of contact refers to the spot where the ball is struck in relation to the center of the clubface. Its primary effect is distance, with a secondary effect on direction. We know that sweet feeling and sound when we hit in the center of the

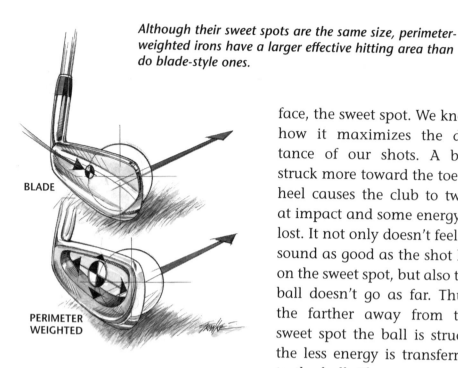

Although their sweet spots are the same size, perimeter-weighted irons have a larger effective hitting area than do blade-style ones.

BLADE

PERIMETER
WEIGHTED

face, the sweet spot. We know how it maximizes the distance of our shots. A ball struck more toward the toe or heel causes the club to twist at impact and some energy is lost. It not only doesn't feel or sound as good as the shot hit on the sweet spot, but also the ball doesn't go as far. Thus, the farther away from the sweet spot the ball is struck, the less energy is transferred to the ball. The sweet spot is only the size of a pinhead. The new clubs on the market do not have a bigger sweet spot. Instead, they have a larger area of what is referred to as an "effective hitting area," which widens the area on the face to allow for shots missed away from the center in order to maximize the energy transfer from the club to the ball. This area is what gives the club a more "forgiving" effect. Nowadays, nearly all drivers and fairway metals are designed to be more friendly to off-center face hits. It's also the reason why "blade"-style irons, which have a smaller effective hitting area, are recommended for more skilled players who tend to hit the ball closer to the center of the face, as opposed to perimeter-weighted "cavity back" irons that are designed to be more forgiving for the average and higher-handicap player.

3. Path. The path is the approach the clubhead takes as it nears the ball. The path of the club has a primary effect on direction, with a secondary effect on distance. The three basic clubhead paths can be described, relative to the target line, as inside out, outside in, and inside-square-inside. The inside-square-inside path is considered the model and is the most natural, as a golf club is designed for us to use

The three basic clubhead paths relative to the target line.

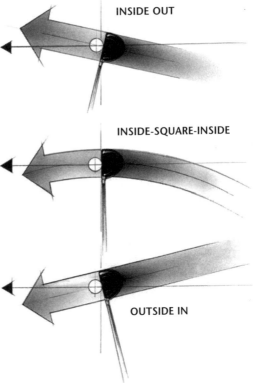

INSIDE OUT

INSIDE-SQUARE-INSIDE

OUTSIDE IN

standing to the side of the ball, parallel to the target line, when we swing the club.

4. Face Angle. The face angle refers to where the face of the club is pointing at impact relative to the target line. Its primary effect is direction, with a secondary effect on distance. The club at impact can be pointing left of the target (closed), right of the target (open), or at the target (square). Since we stand to the side of the ball and the most natural movement of the clubhead is inside-square-inside as we swing the club on an arc, the most natural movement of the clubface is from open (to the right), to square, to closed (to the left). In addition, a golf club is designed for the sweet spot to rotate around the hosel of the club.

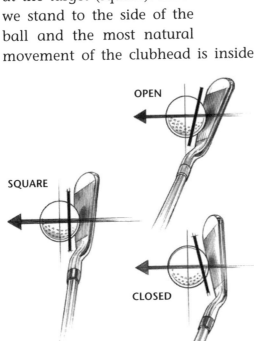

OPEN

SQUARE

CLOSED

The three clubface positions at impact relative to the target line. Open (to the right), square (at the target), and closed (to the left).

The angle of approach is the angle at which the clubhead moves down as it approaches the ground.

5. Angle of Approach. The angle of approach is the angle at which the clubhead moves down as it approaches the ground. The primary effect is distance, with a secondary effect on direction. The steeper the angle of approach the clubhead takes, the more spin will be imparted on the golf ball. Because of the more upright lie angle, shorter clubs are naturally designed to move more steeply than longer clubs.

Look at the chart on the next page that illustrates the nine ball flight patterns.

I have incorporated them into a baseball diamond to provide reference points as I continue this discussion. You need to imagine that center field is more like 300 yards, as opposed to 400 feet. All flights are relative to the target line, which, in this illustration, is a straight line over second base into center field.

To better improve your ball flight, you first need to identify your dominant ball flight pattern. Take a look at the nine ball flights on the opposite page and focus on the two that are on both sides of the straight shot: the straight slice and the straight hook. Which one of the two most resembles your ball flight when the ball starts out straight at the target (center field) and then curves away from the target? I realize some of you are saying "my ball goes everywhere; all nine of these ball flights could be mine." But if you think about it, one of these two patterns is more dominant and a reflection of your ball flight. If you choose the straight slice, for the sake of discussion in this book, you're a slicer, and if you choose the straight hook, you're a hooker. Just to confirm your dominant ball flight, here's another way to find out. If you slice the ball, a push-hook flight pattern is not a shot you would hit, and, conversely, if you hook the ball, a pull-slice flight pattern is not a shot you would hit. If you identify your ball

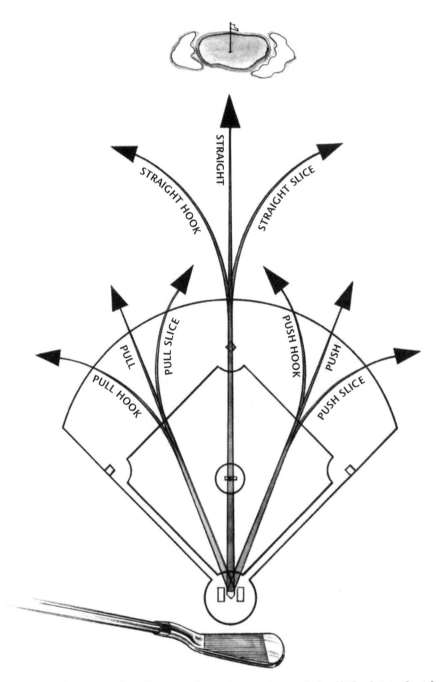

flight as the straight slice, as I go through each ball flight individually, you need to focus on the movement of the club in a straight hook, paying particular attention to what the club is doing in a push hook. If you identify your ball flight as the straight hook, you need to focus on the movement of the club in a straight slice, paying particular attention to what the club is doing in a pull slice. Don't skip over some of the ball flights that you think don't apply to you; you still need to understand all nine flight patterns. However, the reason you should pay particular attention to the flight patterns that you don't hit is that learning the extreme opposite ball flight than the one you normally hit will help you gain a better understanding of the relationship between the club and the ball. In addition, as you work on trying to produce these ball flights, it forces you to exaggerate different elements while exploring, experiencing, and understanding their impact on the ball flight laws. Once you can perform both ball flights, you can balance out the ball flight, work on hitting it straighter or with less curvature, and then decide which one you prefer to play as your "regular" shot. And while the ball flight laws are nonnegotiable, the ball flight you choose to play is negotiable.

Now that you've identified your dominant ball flight pattern, look more closely at each pattern. With these patterns, we'll focus on the two biggest laws, the two that I work on with nearly all of my students. When combined and perfected, they can produce dramatically improved results, similar to the one in the story I shared in the

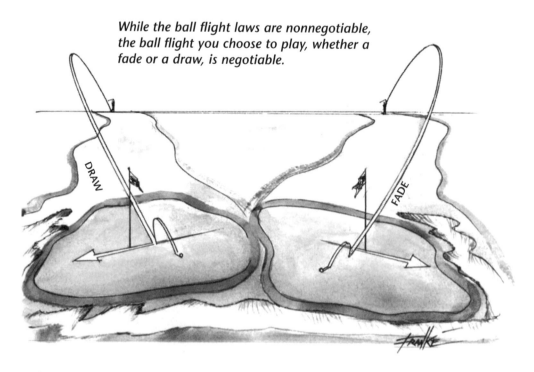

While the ball flight laws are nonnegotiable, the ball flight you choose to play, whether a fade or a draw, is negotiable.

DRAW

FADE

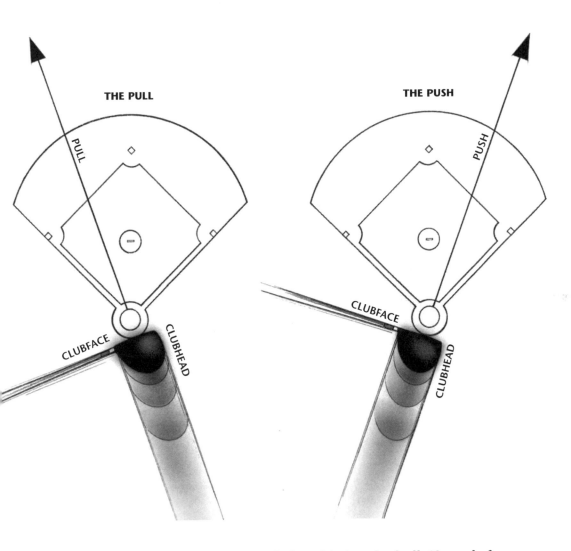

Introduction of the golfer who ended up hitting the ball 60 yards farther with his driver. Those laws are clubface angle and clubhead path. Look first at two patterns that are straight with no curvature. These patterns are defined as a pull and a push. The pull has the ball starting over the shortstop, continuing straight with no curvature, and then continuing straight into left center field. Conversely, the push has the ball starting straight over the second baseman and continuing straight into right center field. These ball flight patterns are the simplest to understand, with the clubhead path and clubface angle moving in the same direction through impact, thereby producing a shot with no curvature.

The third hole at Indian Hills is where I finally learned my lesson about ball flight.

CLUBHEAD

CLUBFACE

My learning experience, and true understanding of ball flight and how curvature happens, started on the third hole at Indian Hills Country Club. It's a par three with very steep bunkers on the right side. A hill rises on the left side of the green and the green slopes severely from left to right. My strategy for the tee shot was to have the ball start at the left side of the green and fade back to the pin. I used the commonly accepted and taught method: "Aim the clubface at the target, align your body where you want the ball to start, and then swing the clubhead across the target line and along your body lines." The problem I was having was that more times than not when I hit the shot, it would start at the flag or just left of it, curve to the right, and land in the bunker. Frustrated with constantly hitting it in the bunker, I would bail out on this strategy and just aim to the left side of the green, toward the hill, and let the ball feed down to the right. But then I would return to the fade strategy, because I was convinced that at my skill level I should be able to play a basic fade shot with a mid-iron. However, I couldn't execute the shot with any level of consistency and many times the ball would wind up going in the bunker on a fly. I went back and forth with these strategies, never really understanding what was going on or why I couldn't execute this shot.

Then, I discovered when reading one of Michael Hebron's books that the face angle has a much more dominant effect on the starting direction of the ball than does the clubhead path. I checked more sources, including my PGA Teaching Manual, to confirm that information. I couldn't believe it. I had always believed that the path of the club was what determined the starting direction of the ball. Now I understood why I kept hitting it in the bunker. The ball was starting fairly close to where I was aiming the clubface, but then, because my path was swinging left of that line, where I was aligning my body, the ball was curving into the bunker.

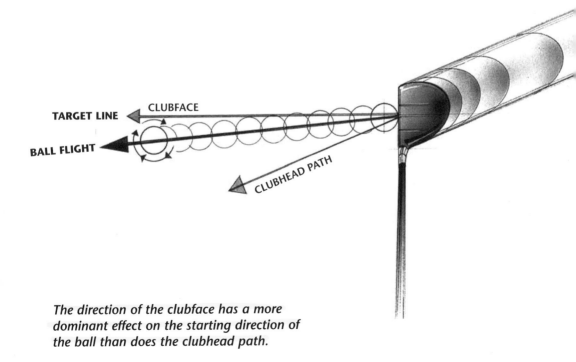

The direction of the clubface has a more dominant effect on the starting direction of the ball than does the clubhead path.

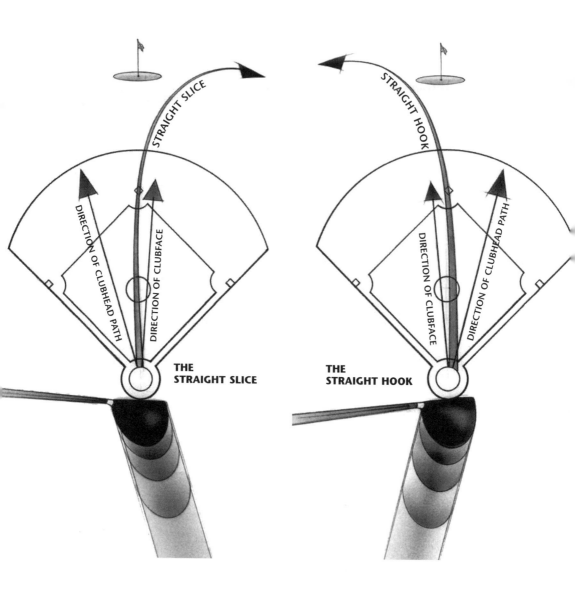

THE
STRAIGHT SLICE

THE
STRAIGHT HOOK

Now that we've established that the face has a much greater influence over the starting direction of the shot than does the path, look next at the patterns of two ball flights that have curvature above, the clubhead path and the clubface angle moving in different directions through impact. These two ball flight patterns are the straight slice and the straight hook. The straight slice has the ball starting over second base, but then curves toward right field. The straight hook does the opposite, starting straight and then curving toward left field. Here, you can see a difference between the direction in which the clubhead is swinging and the direction in which the clubface is pointing when the ball leaves the clubface, and the results of the differential. With the straight slice, the clubface is looking to the right of second base, but the clubhead is swinging toward the shortstop. If you are a hooker, pay particular attention to the movement and position of the clubhead and clubface through impact in the straight slice. The movement of the clubhead path and clubface angle is what you need to work on in order to balance out your ball flight. With the straight hook, the clubface is looking to the left of second base, but the clubhead is swinging toward the second baseman. If you are a slicer you need to pay particular attention to the movement and position of the clubhead and clubface through impact in the straight hook. The slice is sometimes called a fade, while the hook is sometimes called a draw. The terms are relative and subject to personal interpretation and definition. You could say a draw is just a small hook and a fade is a small slice. I've had golfers tell me they are fading the ball with their driver and I see them hit a shot and the ball is curving 20 yards. To me, that's a slice. However, for our discussion, they are one and the same; a ball that draws and a ball that hooks are synonymous, and a ball that fades and one that slices are the same. The former (for a right-handed player) curves to the left and the latter curves to the right.

Two other ball flight patterns start right of the target and curve in a direction. These two are a push slice and a push hook shown on page 62. Both ball flights start out flying toward the second baseman, with the push slice curving toward right field and the push hook curving toward center field. The push slice has the clubface looking at the second baseman, and the clubhead swinging to a point that is more toward second base. The push hook also has the clubface looking at the second baseman, but the clubhead is swinging more toward the first baseman. Although the push hook is on the extreme spectrum of the ball flights, if you have identified yourself as a slicer, and especially if you hit a pull slice, this is the ball flight I would encourage you to learn to hit.

The last two patterns, along with the straight pull, are the most common for a large percentage of golfers. They are the pull hook and the pull slice shown on page 63. Both ball flights start out flying

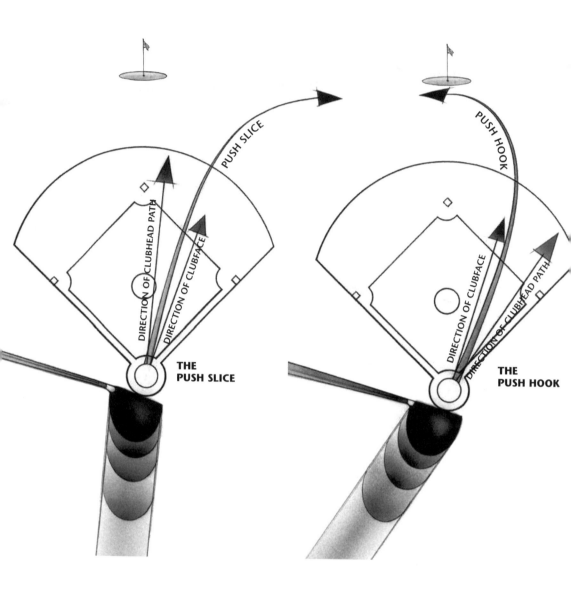

THE PUSH SLICE

THE PUSH HOOK

toward the shortstop, with the pull hook curving toward left field and the pull slice curving toward center field. The pull hook has the clubface looking at the shortstop, but the clubhead is swinging more toward second base. The pull slice, probably the most common ball flight for golfers, has the clubface looking at the shortstop, but the clubhead is swinging more toward the third baseman. The pull slice is on the other extreme spectrum of the ball flights. If you have identified yourself as a hooker, and especially if you hit a push hook, I would encourage you to learn this ball flight.

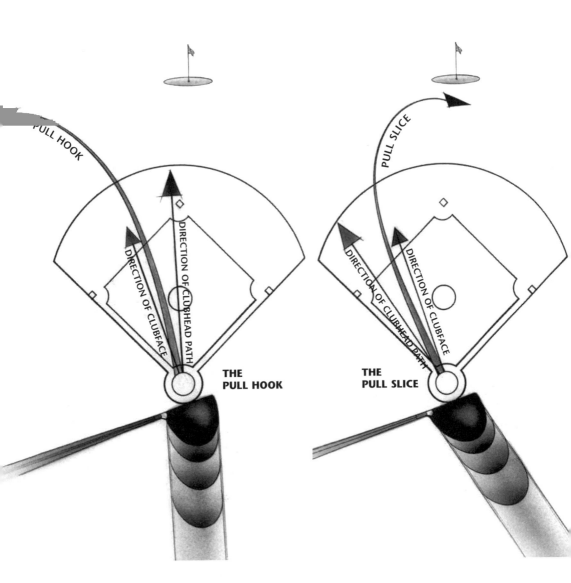

THE
PULL HOOK

THE
PULL SLICE

We've now reviewed eight basic ball flight patterns. All other flights are just lesser or greater degrees of direction and curvature. When the difference between the clubface and clubhead becomes greater, it increases the amount of sidespin on the ball, which in turn increases the curvature on ball flight.

So what about the ninth ball flight pattern, the elusive straight shot, the ball flight that in the baseball field would go straight over the pitcher, second base, and into center field? Before I answer that question, take a look at the photo on page 64.

Looking at the clock on the ball, with 12:00 being opposite of where you stand and 9:00 facing the target, which part of the clock should the clubface hit at impact? If you are like most golfers, your answer will be 3:00. But golfers who answer 3:00 don't understand impact and separation, a topic that is almost never talked about. The correct answer is 4:00. Let me put a disclaimer on this by saying I don't know exactly where it is on the clock, but it's definitely not 3:00; rather it is on the inner quadrant of the ball. The reason for this is that the club is moving on an arc. The clubface contacts the inner quadrant of the ball, closer to the 4:00 position, compresses on the face for a split second, and then comes off the face at a different position, ideally at 3:00, producing a straight shot. I'm not fond of tidbits of information being suggested in the form of general tips, but if there's one single truth in golf that I have shared with golfers that has had the greatest impact in helping them stop slicing the ball, it is this expla-

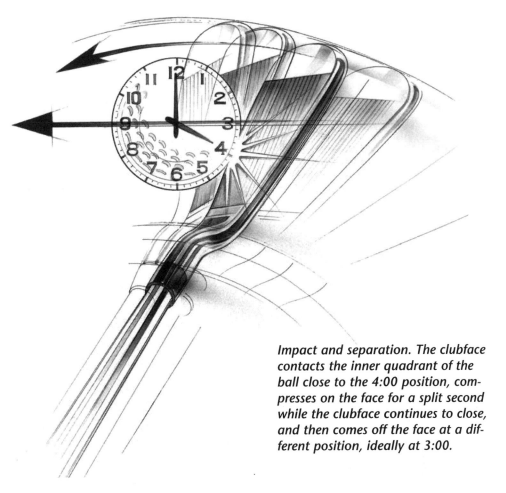

Impact and separation. The clubface contacts the inner quadrant of the ball close to the 4:00 position, compresses on the face for a split second while the clubface continues to close, and then comes off the face at a different position, ideally at 3:00.

nation of impact and separation. Another interesting fact that most golfers are not aware of is that during the process of impact and separation, the clubhead actually slows down by about 20%. However, I didn't include the information about impact and separation in the above examples when I discussed all of the ball flights. Why? Simply because when one starts to explain impact and separation with all of

The ball is compressed at impact.

the factors that determine ball flight laws (clubhead path, clubface angle, speed, centeredness of contact, and angle of approach), it just becomes too complicated and much too confusing.

There are other results of basic combinations of factors that produce ball flight laws that most golfers don't understand. Clubhead speed and clubs with different lofts have different effects on ball flight. A player's clubhead speed, for example, affects sidespin and, therefore, curvature of the flight. If you took two players, one who hits a driver 190 yards and the other who hits it 280 yards, you'd see a significant difference in the amount the ball curves away from its starting point. The faster the player moves the club, the more sidespin is imparted on the ball, even though the relationship and difference between the clubface and clubhead are identical for both players. Players who are very powerful and hit the ball long could pay the bigger penalty when the shot goes astray. If both players sliced the ball with the identical clubface direction and clubhead path, the shorter hitter may be in the right side of the fairway, whereas the longer hitter may be deep in the right woods. Once I was giving a lesson to a golfer who was hitting a big slice. At the end of the lesson, the student started talking about techniques on the downswing to get more speed and wanted to know when we could start working on improving them so that he could hit the ball farther. I explained that we first needed to get the ball going straight, and then we could work on speed. With more speed, he would just hit it farther into the woods.

Each club in your bag has a different degree of loft. More lofted clubs, like the short irons, create more backspin and, in turn, have a different effect on the flight of the ball. I often hear how golfers are satisfied with their ball flight from their wedge to their seven iron, but not with how the ball flight starts to become unmanageable as the club they are hitting with gets longer, and how the ball flight is really magnified and out of control with their driver. I once observed Mike Mangiaracina, a fellow PGA Professional, give a lesson to a golfer. The student was hitting some balls with a nine iron on the driving range. Mike watched him hit balls for a couple of minutes before the guy turned to Mike and asked him what he thought. Mike told him to get rid of that "liar," and handed him a five iron. What Mike was saying was that the short irons don't tell the truth. And he's right, for two

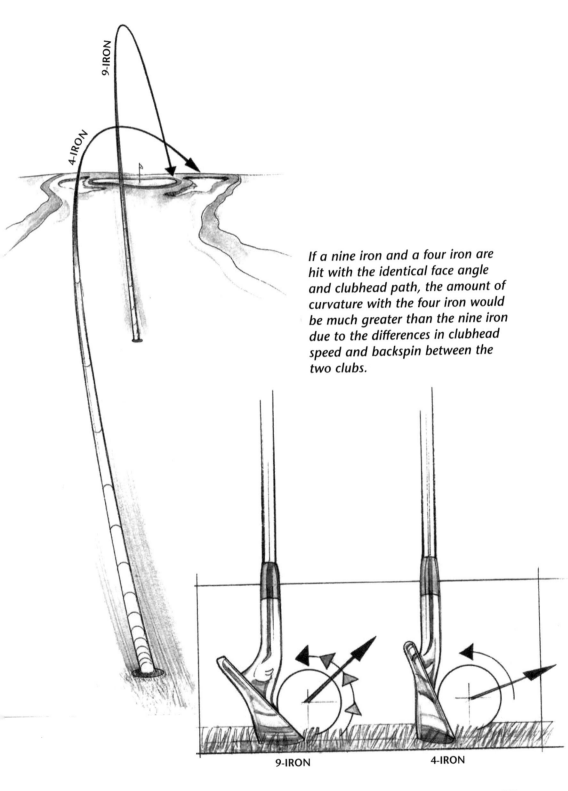

9-IRON

4-IRON

If a nine iron and a four iron are hit with the identical face angle and clubhead path, the amount of curvature with the four iron would be much greater than the nine iron due to the differences in clubhead speed and backspin between the two clubs.

9-IRON

4-IRON

reasons. Short irons move with less speed than longer clubs, imparting much less sidespin than the longer ones. Also, the loft on the short irons and a sharper angle of approach cause more backspin. Backspin offsets sidespin and causes the ball to curve less. If you hit a nine iron and a four iron with the identical face angle and clubhead path, the amount of curvature would be greater with the four iron. Understand that if you are a golfer who curves the ball, in either direction, you actually need the starting direction of the ball, or your alignment, to be different with every club in your bag, since each club will curve a different amount.

I do admit that I have simplified some things from a physics standpoint. However, due to complexities of factoring in all of the laws, I had no choice but to simplify my explanations. For those of you who are very scientifically oriented and want a much more in-depth reading on ball flight, including discussions on ballistics and vectors along with a lot of scientific data on the golf swing, I suggest three books: *Search For the Perfect Swing, The Golfing Machine,* and *The Physics of Golf.*

Most golfers need to make a change with both their swing path and their face angle to improve their ball flight. This is an important point and the reason why many golfers fail to improve their ball flight. Many times only changing the clubhead path or the clubface angle through impact will not produce better results. More times than not, it's a two-part solution.

The slicer needs to get the clubhead approaching the ball from more of an inside path. Conversely, the hooker needs to get the clubhead approaching the ball from more of an outside path. However, many times changing the clubhead path has an impact on the face angle, where the face is pointing, at impact. In other words, those of you who have been hitting a pull may say that your clubface is already closed relative to the target line because the clubface is pointing to left field, but this may change once your clubhead path is changed. Of course, the same is true for golfers who hook the ball. When you change your path, it will most likely change your face angle. In addition, the path of the clubhead when it travels from outside in tends to promote an opening of the clubface, whereas an inside-out path tends to cause a closing of the clubface.

When changing your swing path, it can be helpful to use the baseball diamond as a visual to make the clubhead swing toward a specific spot in the field. This method seems to work for many golfers. However, when I help golfers change their swing path, the most successful solution I have ever shared is based on the "clock on the ball" image. If you hit a slice, you need to work on hitting the ball more from the inside by aiming to hit 4:00 in order to produce a more inside path for the clubhead. If that still doesn't produce the ball flight you are looking for, aim more toward 5:00. If you hook the ball, start aiming to hit 2:00 and, if necessary, 1:00. If results are too exaggerated on either side of the ball, both hookers and slicers can start working their way back toward 3:00. Fine-tune and dial into the area on the clock that works best for you.

Use the image of the clock on the ball to help you visualize the clubhead path you want to swing the club on.

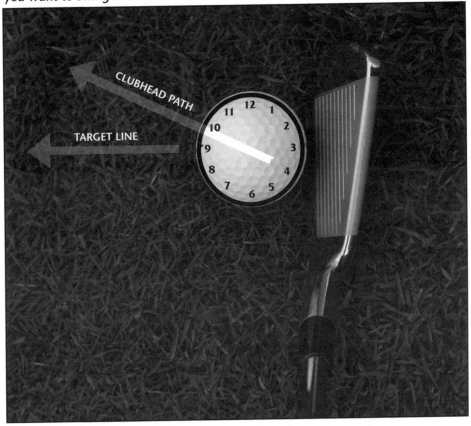

Experimenting with extremes puts you in touch with reality, which is a key ingredient in making changes. I personally use this idea on my own game. I tend to swing the clubhead too much from the inside at times, hitting big pushes and hooks. One way I work to move the club more outside on the downswing is to try to hit the ball at 2:00. Sometimes it feels like I'm swinging at 2:00 and the club is still coming too much from the inside. Then, I work on hitting 1:30, and keep dialing in until I find the spot on the clock, the correct swing path, that allows my ball to fly with little curvature in either direction. Once I get the sensation I need to produce the path I'm looking for, I no longer focus on the spot on the ball, but rather on the feeling of the overall movement of the golf club. When you perform this exercise, don't get caught up in the exact positions on the clock and impact and separation, because it will drive you crazy. Just make general observations and adjustments.

You can also use striped range balls to help change your ball flight. Set the stripe in the direction of the path you want to swing the clubhead and swing down that line. Another method to give you feedback so that you can better understand your ball flight pattern and monitor your swing path is to tie a piece of ribbon or thin strip of light cloth, two to three feet long, to the hosel of the club. I picked up this idea back in 1999, watching Craig Shainkland give a presentation at the PGA Teaching Summit. You can take practice swings or actually hit balls with

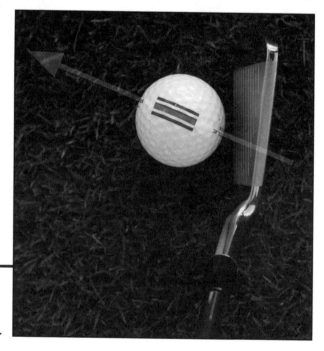

Use the stripe on a range ball to help you visualize the clubhead path you want to swing the club on.

the ribbon on the club. The color "trail" that is left behind visually provides feedback as to the path of the clubhead. Another exercise to help reshape your clubhead path is to use a head cover, golf ball, or another object. The goal is to try not to hit the object, which will give you visual feedback. Using a tee is one of the simplest objects to utilize for this exercise. You can use tees whether practicing on grass or on mats; the difference is that on the mats the rubber tee is fixed and won't move, but you should receive audible feedback if you hit it. If you are trying to learn to swing the club more from the inside, place the tee so it's positioned

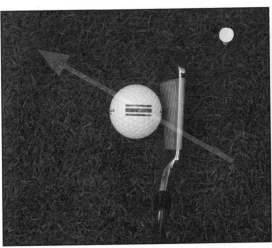 

Position a tee, or other small object, just outside the clubhead and avoid hitting it when striking the ball to help encourage the particular path you are working on.

just outside the clubhead and slightly behind the ball. If you swing from the outside, the clubhead will strike the tee. To stop a hook, place the tee so its position is just outside the clubhead and slightly in front of the ball. When doing these exercises and correcting your path, use at least a seven iron, preferably a six or five iron, and ultimately test your progress with the driver or three wood (three metal).

I cannot stress enough the importance of the material in this chapter. As golfers, we understand that the more controllable and predictable our ball flight is, the better we can play. But you must understand the principles of ball flight and the effects the club has on the ball in order to make the proper changes and adjustments to your own golf swing. If you don't understand ball flight, it is like being blindfolded and wearing earplugs on the basketball court, throwing up balls in hopes that you'll make a shot. If necessary, keep rereading this chapter until you understand every part of it. With your understanding of ball flight patterns and the nonnegotiable laws governing them, you can next learn the negotiable elements of direction and distance to improve your ability to control the flight of your ball.

CHAPTER 5

Swing Plane and the Elements of the Right Side

This chapter focuses on swing plane and the elements of the right side that influence it, all of which have a primary effect on direction, with a secondary effect on distance. But remember, more times than not, improving the directional elements and laws also leads to increased distance. In the last chapter, I gave you some suggestions on changing the swing path and face angle of your golf club by solely focusing on the movement of the golf club. In this chapter, you will find more suggestions to help you improve your swing path by working on your swing plane, along with explanations to help you understand how the elements related to the right side of the body influence the movement of the golf club.

One of the most talked about things in golf is the swing plane. Each club has a lie angle, which is what determines the swing plane. When drawn as a visual, the swing plane is a line drawn through the shaft at address and continuing up at the same angle. *Therefore, since every club has a different lie angle, the swing plane varies with the lie angle of the club.* Much emphasis is placed on the importance of swing plane, but it is often explained in different ways and is confused with swing path. Swing plane refers to the movement of the clubshaft throughout the swing relative to the original plane line established at address, whereas swing path refers to the movement of the clubhead relative to the target line. The primary influence of swing plane is on the clubhead path. The discussion of swing plane can become very confusing when combined with swing path, as it often is. Therefore, I've simplified it by eliminating some of the possible combinations that can exist between them and focusing more on the most common combinations.

First, look at how the club moves with the ideal model downswing plane. Early in the downswing, for the club to be on the ideal plane line, or "on plane," the clubshaft plane line is parallel to and above the original plane line. Notice that the butt of the club is pointing outside the target line, not at the target line as is often explained. As the club moves down to where it is parallel to the ground, it is also parallel to the target line. This is the point where the clubhead gets back on the original plane line and then moves through the bottom half of its arc. Note that because it is not on the plane line until it gets to this point, the shaft has actually been traveling down toward the original plane line and is going through many planes. The club is not moving on one plane, but rather multiple plane lines that ideally are parallel to the original plane line. At impact, the shaft of the club matches up with the original position of the club at address. When the shaft of the club moves through these points, the clubhead is on the natural path established by the club's original design, which is inside-square-inside.

Below: *When drawn as a visual, the swing plane is a line that's determined by the lie angle of the clubshaft and continues up at the same angle.* Center: *Since the lie angle is different on each club, so is the swing plane.*

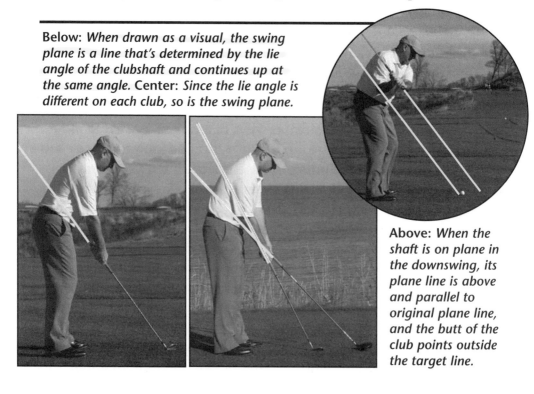

Above: *When the shaft is on plane in the downswing, its plane line is above and parallel to original plane line, and the butt of the club points outside the target line.*

Left: *When the club is parallel to the ground, it is also parallel to the target line.* Right: *At impact the clubshaft matches up with its original position.*

Several in-swing elements impact swing plane. If I had to isolate a single area on the body that has the most influence on swing plane and clubhead path, it would be, for right-handed golfers, what I refer to as the right side system. This system includes the right shoulder, elbow, forearm, wrist, and hand. The right shoulder is what I consider the core of the system; it has a major influence on swing plane and therefore on the path the clubhead takes on the downswing. When the shoulder goes down and under, the club will follow the shoulder's

From the top of the backswing (1), the right shoulder moves downward (2) and puts the club on plane (3).

The right shoulder continues to move down through impact.

movement and move down toward the ideal plane and path. When I say "down" with the right shoulder, I'm not referring to the dropping of the body, but rather the path the shoulder is taking on the downswing. There is more evidence of the downward path of the right shoulder when you observe the position and shoulder plane angle of accomplished players just at and through impact. However, when the shoulder moves out and around, more toward the target line, the club follows it, moves farther away from the original plane line, and the path of the club goes outside and creates an outside-in swing path. However, a player who moves the shoulder down at too steep an angle could make the club drop under the plane line, causing the clubhead to approach the ball excessively from the inside and creating an inside-out clubhead path. The path the right shoulder takes influences the direction that the arms and the club take; in

From the top of the backswing (1), if the right shoulder starts to go out and around (2), the club will follow (3), resulting in a clubhead path that will be outside in (4).

essence, it is the beginning of the right side system. First, the shoulder moves, then the upper arm, elbow, forearm, and, finally, the wrist, hand, and then the golf club. *It can be very helpful for a golfer to think about the movement of his or her shoulder at the start of the downswing.* A golfer who slices the ball and has an outside-in swing path will probably benefit from feeling the shoulder go down, but this may be damaging for a golfer who has an inside-out swing path and hooks the ball. He or she may be better off thinking about the shoulder going out and around. However, all golfers may also find it more helpful to focus on the movement of other body parts in the right side system, as opposed to the right shoulder, to change the swing plane and path of the club on the downswing.

Negotiable Element—
THE RIGHT ELBOW

The right elbow can have a major impact on the plane the club travels on the downswing. Many times you'll hear the suggestion "Don't let the right elbow fly at the top." This refers to an elbow position that is high, above the right shoulder and behind the player's torso. But what does that mean and how does it affect the club? If the right elbow is in this position at the top of the backswing and is not changed at the start of the downswing, the shaft is too vertical (steep) and will produce an outside-in swing path. Therefore, all accomplished players who play with a high right elbow position make the necessary downswing adjustment with their right arm of moving the

When the elbow is in a high position (1), it is behind the body, and if no other adjustment is made (2) the club will travel on an outside-in path (3).

From the top of his backswing Fred Couples makes the necessary elbow adjustment on his downswing to put the club back on plane.

elbow so that the right forearm becomes perpendicular to the ground, with the elbow now pointing down to the ground. This puts the golf club back into more effective position. The more conventional position for the elbow at the top is a position where it is pointing down and in front of the body, which is considered a more efficient position because it allows for a simpler transition to get the club on plane in the downswing.

Because preventing the high-flying elbow position is a concern of many golfers, they try to keep the right elbow close to the body. This concept is often used in an effort to tuck and "connect" the right arm, keeping it pressed against the side of the body, which

Below: *At the top, when the right elbow is down and in front of the body, it makes for a simpler transition to get the club on plane on the downswing.*

Above: *At the top of her backswing, Annika Sorenstam's right forearm is vertical, with her right elbow pointing down to the ground and in front of her body.*

No

Yes

Allow the right elbow to breathe at the top.

The right elbow gets in front of the right hip on the downswing.

Putting objects under the right arm, and/or trying to keep the right arm pinned to the side of the body, prevents the right elbow from getting in front of the right hip on the downswing.

of course prevents the high elbow position. Sometimes drills are employed with towels or headcovers, with these items being placed under the right armpit and held there throughout the swing to keep this so-called connection. This is a poor concept. On the downswing, the right elbow needs to get in front of the right hip. This position is evident and a common denominator in nearly all effective golf swings. When the elbow is pinned to the side at the top, the body gets in the way and blocks the elbow's path on the downswing.

The visual of holding a waiter's tray at the top of the backswing can help a golfer place the right elbow in a more conventional position.

When drawn as a visual, the left arm creates a line, and is defined as being on plane, when it is parallel to the club's plane line. **Below:** At the top of his backswing, Jim Furyk's left arm plane angle is steeper than the club's original plane line angle.

And while it could be said that the more efficient position of the right elbow at the top occurs when it is pointing down, slightly away from and in front of the body, because it does not require any additional adjustments on the downswing, it's certainly not the only way. *Therefore, the position of the right elbow at the top of the swing is negotiable.*

Negotiable Element—THE LEFT ARM POSITION AT THE TOP

Basically, the right arm controls and gives structure to the left arm's position at the top of the swing, directly influencing it. At the top, we can observe the left arm as another plane line angle and see how it relates to the original plane line of the golf club. The higher the right hand is at the top, the steeper or more upright the left arm will be relative to the original plane line. The lower the right hand is, the flatter the left arm will be. Most instructors would agree that the ideal position is when at the top the left arm creates a line parallel to the club's original plane line. However, many great players have their left arm higher (more upright) than this). Generally, the higher the left arm is at the top, the more it has to slide down the chest before it reaches impact. The latest trend is for golfers to adopt one of two styles; that of either a one-plane or two-plane swinger. Basically, a player whose left arm is parallel to the original plane line is now classified as a one-plane swinger, whereas a player whose left arm is above parallel is considered a two-plane swinger.

Players have been playing from these different positions since the birth of the game. My issue with these types of concepts is that they

The late, great ball-striker Ben Hogan had his left arm at the top of his swing below the plane line.

place golfers in categories and encourage them to do one thing or another. Without the monitoring of a professional, this categorization is dangerous and for some it can be counterproductive, for others disastrous. I work with some golfers who have poor flexibility in their left shoulder and can't get their arms up high enough to be parallel to the original plane line. Does this mean that these golfers are doomed to poor golf for life because they can't fit into one of these models? The late Ben Hogan, one of the greatest ball strikers the game has ever seen, played with his left arm in a position lower (flatter) than the left arm being parallel to the original plane line.

Great players throughout the decades of time have played with their left arms in positions other than the one exhibited in the model. *Therefore, the position of the left arm at the top of the swing is negotiable.*

Negotiable Element—BACKSWING PLANE

So what about the plane of the club on the backswing? Some instructors contend that on the backswing the shaft should be steeper than the original plane line. Thereby if you extended the visual line of the club to the ground, it would point inside the target line. I don't agree. It doesn't make sense

Ernie Els has the clubshaft on a steeper plane angle than the original plane angle on his backswing, then flattens the shaft on the downswing so it is parallel and on plane.

Golfers can benefit from visualizing the backswing plane slightly above, but parallel to, the original plane line angle.

John Daly takes the club back under the original plane line, then, on the downswing puts the club back on plane.

that the club should move up on a plane angle that is not parallel to the original plane line only to shift back to a parallel position on the downswing. Certainly, there are accomplished golfers who move the club in this manner on the backswing. Some do it just because it feels natural to them; others because they were guided by their instructors to employ this method. They are world-class athletes, however, and I honestly believe that if they had been instructed to take the club back so that it's parallel to the plane line, they would have been just as successful. When a golfer visualizes his or her backswing plane, my preference is that it would be parallel to the original shaft plane, with the butt of the club pointing outside the target line, and not at the target line, as is often explained. Nevertheless, backswing planes, and the path the clubhead takes on the backswing, are especially negotiable since you don't hit the ball on the backswing. The golf ball does not respond to your backswing, only to your downswing. Most golfers are told that in order to have an effective downswing, they must

TIGER WOODS   JIM FURYK

From setup to impact, players can move the club very differently, yet still have effective golf swings.

have a model-like, on-plane backswing. However, the best players in the world do it differently. Some do take it back on plane, but others take the club below (under) or well above the plane line on the backswing, and then put the club back on plane in the downswing.

One problem is that many golfers randomly change the backswing plane or path of their clubhead because they are hitting the ball poorly. They equate a bad golf shot with a bad backswing. But I've seen golfers change their backswing to improve their ball-striking when their backswing is perfectly fine, changing it for the worse. The backswing should only be changed if it is negatively impacting the downswing. Sure, the backswing is going to impact the position of the arms and club at the top, which in turn will impact the downswing, but backswing changes can't be random and without purpose. It's fine

to experiment with different backswing ideas, as long as you understand how they impact the downswing movement of the golf club.
Then, you can evaluate whether one method is better than another
for your swing. The path and plane the club takes on the backswing
is negotiable.

The important point that needs to be understood about the movement of the golf club and the body going back, to the top, and down
to impact, is that even when observing the swings of world-class players, the clubhead path can be dramatically different from player to
player, yet still produce an effective swing that, in turn, produces a
consistent, predictable ball flight.

To be honest, I was reluctant about including much of the information in this chapter for several reasons. The primary reason is the
challenge of self-monitoring. This is why I don't like golfers trying to
focus on ideas such as being a one-plane or two-plane swinger. How
do you know which one you are? The challenge with focusing on
swing plane, on the backswing or downswing, and the movements
and positions of your right side, is that it is very difficult to self-mon-
itor the position of your body or the clubshaft throughout the swing,
when you are actually hitting the ball, without the help of video or
another person watching. In the end, however, I felt that this discussion about these areas of the swing needed to be included, as there is
so much confusing and conflicting information within the golfing
community.

With all this being said, if you are
not going to seek help from a qualified
golf professional, and you want to
explore these ideas on your own, here
are suggestions that will, at the very
least, provide a source of feedback.

One method that can help you
monitor your swing plane when you are
practicing is to have a friend stand

*For feedback, have a friend kneel down
behind you with a club, and visually match
up the clubshaft to the club's original shaft
plane angle.*

Understand and practice the movement of the clubshaft by positioning a piece of tape on a full-length mirror so that it traces the club's original plane line angle created by the clubshaft at address.

behind you with a club, and have him or her use the club to mirror your shaft at address. As you hit balls, he or she can give you feedback as to the position of the shaft on the backswing and downswing.

If working by yourself, a mirror can be a very helpful way to visualize swing plane and specific body elements and positions, such as the position of your right elbow at the top of the backswing and its influence on the movement of the clubshaft relative to the original plane line. Using a full-length mirror, put a club up against the mirror and trace a line with non-clear tape, matching the line with the shaft angle of the club. Next, step far enough away from the mirror so that you can take a swing. When you look back at the mirror, you want to be in a position where the line of tape matches your clubshaft angle. Now you have a reference point and a source of feedback as to how the shaft looks, relative to the original plane angle, when you move it in your swing. Focus on the movement of the shaft back and through the swing, stopping

Common denominators in effective swings; right elbow in front of body and pointing down, clubshaft on plane.

in different positions, and try to match the plane lines (the shaft should be parallel to the tape line) on the backswing and downswing. Most importantly, focus on getting the club on plane with both elbows in front of you, with the right elbow pointing down to the ground and the clubshaft on plane—a position you see with all great players. What's interesting is that many times when I get a player to understand this position, many of the other elements in his or her backswing and at the top of the swing start to change simply as a result of understanding where the club needs to be on the downswing. Experiment with different body positions and their influence on the club. Interestingly, if you focus solely on the movement and positions of the golf club, you will see the body elements changing into what can be more effective positions; again, form following function.

CHAPTER 6

Direction and the
Pre-Swing Elements

Now that you have an understanding of the movement of the golf club and its effect on the direction of the flight of the golf ball, focus on the things you do before you put the club in motion: the pre-swing elements, commonly referred to as the setup. These elements are posture, alignment, grip, and ball position. They have a primary influence on direction, with a secondary influence on distance. In this chapter, you will learn how these negotiable elements can help you improve your swing path and face angle and understand how the pre-swing elements influence the movement of the golf club.

As I mentioned before, although focusing on changing your swing path alone may be enough, you may also need to change your clubface angle at impact. Therefore, keep in mind as you read these chapters that you may also have to change other elements, such as your grip, to change your face angle. You may need to change your alignment along with your swing path, or sometimes a ball position change may be all you need to adjust your swing path. You'll need to experiment to find the compatible arrangement of elements that work for you.

The pre-swing elements are usually the last elements to be looked at when diagnosing inconsistent or uncontrollable ball flight. The lack of attention that golfers give to these areas has always been a mystery to me. The pre-swing elements are universally discussed in every golf book and magazine, yet most of the average golfers I see have poor setups. I believe that golfers are aware that these elements are important, but they don't understand why they are important and how they affect the movement of the body and the golf club. As I said, the primary challenge golfers face is that they can't see themselves; therefore, it also becomes more difficult to experience the proper setup fundamentals. Without outside feedback, it's difficult to make improvement changes and monitor them. In addition, all golfers have some successful days despite possessing poor pre-swing fundamentals. However, many times the good days are because the subconscious mind is making necessary minute compensations and adjustments to offset errors in the golfer's setup and swing. When things go wrong, the fundamentals of the setup may be the last place golfers look to fix the problem. They are more likely to overlook their grip or posture and instead focus on the movement of their head, left

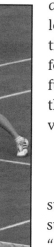

arm, or some other body part as the problem. However, just as a house has a foundation, the pre-swing fundamentals are the foundation of your golf swing. Without a fundamentally solid foundation, eventually things will crumble to the ground. Or at the very least, struggle to stay up.

Negotiable Element—POSTURE

Many incomplete and misunderstood suggestions with regard to posture abound, such as "Set up in an athletic position," or "Bend your knees," or "Set up like you're standing up and sitting on a barstool." Many golfers are misled and misinterpret these ideas. An athletic position for sports such as

A "ready" position for other sports, such as tennis and baseball, requires more knee bend than the set-up position in golf.

Above: *Proper posture has spine tilt created from bending at the hips; the lower back is relatively straight, the knees are slightly flexed, and the arms are hanging relaxed from the shoulders.* **Right:** *Many golfers have a bent-over posture, excessively curving the spine.*

basketball, baseball, or tennis is different than it is for golf. When playing many other sports, we need to quickly step laterally, forward and backward, and many times jump off the ground. None of these movements are necessary for golf.

Thinking about their knees and flexing them excessively in an attempt to have better balance and stability is the primary reason why most golfers have poor posture. A focus on the knees affects the spine angle. When golfers set up with the proper spine angle, the lower back is relatively straight, with the bend coming from the hips, as opposed to the waist and excessively curving the spine. Some golfers believe that it's necessary to straighten the upper part of the back, but I believe this is unnatural as most of us have a slight curvature at the top of the spine. Making an effort to do this can cause tension to build in the shoulders. So what does this spine angle do for our golf swing? It actually does several very important things. The first is that it allows your arms to hang from your shoulders at address, thereby relaxing them, and, as most golfers know, relaxation in the arms can be helpful. The second thing that proper spine angle does is allow the shoulders to turn on a more effective angle, thereby making it easier to swing the arms and the club on plane.

To avoid a bobbing effect, the spine angle needs to be maintained in the backswing.

Proper spine angle allows the shoulders to turn, not too vertical or horizontal, thereby making it easier to swing the arms and club on plane.

Maintaining that angle from setup to impact is very important. If a player loses his or her spine angle in the backswing, or what is referred to as "standing up," he or she will then have to make a downward movement and increase the angle on the downswing. This movement becomes a bobbing effect, with the player moving up in the backswing and down in the forward swing. The amount the player stands up in the backswing creates a greater need for compensation on the downswing to offset the movement in the backswing. If the error, so to speak, is not offset precisely by the compensation, the player will inevitably struggle to make consistent contact with the ball. I have this particular problem. I stand up a little on the backswing and sometimes I compound this error by moving down too much on the downswing, effectively bringing my upper body closer to the ball. This creates the need for another compensation; now I have to "shorten" my arms, bring them in closer to my body by bending them at impact to offset that error. When this happens, my ball-striking can really suffer. This is also a classic example of the domino effect of errors and compensations.

When the knees are excessively bent, the upper torso is too vertical (right) and will cause the shoulders to turn horizontally, moving the club off plane in the early part of the backswing (below).

When a golfer bends the knees first, there is no room for the proper spine angle to be created. This forces the golfer to reach for the ball, and can cause excessive tension in the arms. If there is an inadequate degree of spine angle at address, the golfer will have more difficulty in swinging the club on plane going back. Because of the lack of angle, the golfer will tend to rotate the shoulders on a very horizontal plane, causing him or her to move the club inside on the backswing, well under the plane, or lift the arms in an effort to avoid it, both of which can make creating an effective downswing more difficult. I have to constantly monitor my spine angle with video or a mirror, because like many

Below: *Adequate spine angle is necessary for the right arm and elbow to get in front of the hip on the downswing.* **Right:** *When the upper body has an inadequate amount of spine tilt, the path for the right arm and elbow will be blocked by the body on the downswing.*

golfers I work with, my tendency is to set up with too little angle and to reach for the ball. When I do this I find it much more difficult to swing the club in an effective manner. Another important benefit of adequate spine angle is that it enables the right arm and elbow to get in front of the hip on the downswing. Without the adequate angle, the body blocks the right arm on the downswing. This forces the arms and club to seek a clear path on the downswing, which is usually away from the body, toward the outside, creating an outside-in path.

Understand that every golfer's posture is a little different because of height and the ratio of the upper torso to the length of the legs and arms. Many times taller players have to bend their knees more than shorter players do to get the club down to the ball. This is one of the real benefits of club fitting. Some golfers have clubs that won't allow them to set up correctly. The clubs are either too upright or too flat. It then becomes necessary for the golfers to make unnecessary, ineffective adjustments for their clubs at the address position, and those adjustments cause a poor posture.

Take a look at your posture in a full-length mirror. If, like most players, your posture looks like it needs improvement, try this exer-

A four-point sequence for improved posture. 1. Stand up with your legs very straight and your arms and club extended out in front of you. 2. Keep the lower back straight and bend from the hips, but don't bend your knees. 3. Relax your arms. 4. Slightly flex your knees.

cise. (Photos on page 92) First, stand up with your legs very straight and your arms and club extended out in front of you, and then bend from the hips, but don't bend your knees. Next, relax your arms, and then slightly flex your knees. You want to be balanced, with your weight between the balls and heels of your feet. If you are not balanced with a solid foundation and are leaning either forward toward your toes, or backward toward your heels, your body will need to do what's natural—keep you in balance when you are swinging the club. The good news is your mind won't let you fall over. The bad news is it will be more focused on keeping you in balance, as opposed to swinging the golf club.

The other important angle in the setup has the spine tilting away from the target and the right shoulder being lower than the left. The

The spine tilts slightly away from the target, and the right shoulder is lower than the left.

A posture that has the spine tilting slightly away from the target, and the right shoulder lower than the left, encourages the right shoulder to move downward on the downswing.

Use a full-length mirror as a way to effectively monitor and practice your posture.

shoulder angle is created, in part, as a result of the right hand being lower on the club than the left hand. This posture is also very beneficial in getting the right shoulder to move down on the downswing.

Using a mirror is a very useful and, when by yourself, possibly the only way to learn to improve your posture. Without a mirror or video, you have no visual source of feedback and can easily be misled by your feelings. When I work with a golfer, one of the first things I do is take a still photo of his or her posture, show the photo, discuss some suggestions to improve the posture, and then help implement those changes. Then, I take another picture. Nearly every time, a golfer making a posture change will say that the improved posture feels very awkward. Many times he or she feels very self-conscious when learning to improve the spine angle. Most commonly, he or she feels like his or her rear end is sticking out. However, when I show the golfer a picture of the new posture, the golfer can't believe how normal it looks versus how odd and awkward it feels.

Even though a player's physical attributes contribute to his or her posture, when you observe good players with similar physical attributes, you'll still see some differences from player to player. Some have more knee bend while others have more spine angle. The important thing is to find the posture that helps you swing the club in an effective way that works for you. *Posture is negotiable.*

Negotiable Element—ALIGNMENT

There is a difference between alignment and aim. Golfers and instructors use the words "aim" and "alignment" differently, with aim sometimes referring to the clubface and alignment referring to the position of the body. When I say "aim," I'm referring to the intended target, whereas "alignment" is the direction the clubface is pointing at address, along with where the body (the shoulders, hips, knees, and feet) are aligned relative to the target line. It's common for a player to be aimed at an intended point where he or she wants the ball to go, for example, the flagstick, and be aligned to a different point, say the bunker that is to the right of the green. One time when I was working with a golfer, we were talking about tour players and he commented that he wished he could swing like Tiger Woods. Jokingly, I told him Tiger Wood's swing is based on where he is aimed and aligned, and that if he made swings like Woods, he would never get off the first tee, especially at our golf course, which has a boundary fence on the right side of the hole. The reason the golfer would have trouble is that he was aligned considerably to the right of his intended target. Nearly all right-handed golfers I work with align themselves to the right of their intended target, as do I. I've seen golfers align themselves as far as 40 yards off line of their intended target. When golfers come to me for help, I'll pick a target for them. I've seen golfers who hit the ball dead straight to the right of the target and comment that that's the problem they're experiencing. Yet the fact is that they are hitting it exactly to where they were aligned, but they were aligned to the right of the intended target. You don't want to use the model clubhead path to hit the ball straight unless you are aligned to the intended target. If you are aiming at a target but aligned to a different one, you need to make some non-model-like compensations in your swing in order to get the ball to go to the target.

In golf, aligning to the intended target seems to be more difficult than in other sports, but in most other activities, such as throwing a ball or shooting a basketball, you're facing the target. It is very challenging for a golfer to consistently align him or herself; therefore, it is necessary to monitor your alignment. If you go to a professional tour event and watch the players warm up or practice, many of them have clubs or umbrellas on the ground, parallel to their target, to assist them with their alignment. I try to always practice with a club on the

ground to aid me with my alignment. If I get lazy and don't pay attention to my alignment, I start aligning myself too far to the right of my intended target, sometimes as much as ten yards, which, by the way, contributes to my problem of hitting uncontrollable pushes and hooks.

The parallel setup, used by players like Tiger Woods, is considered the model.

Ian Poulter, like many tour players, practices with a club on the ground, parallel to his target line, as an alignment reference.

The model alignment has the feet, hips, knees, and shoulders all running parallel to the target line.

To check your alignment, while in your set-up have someone put a club down indicating where you are aiming the clubface, and another one indicating where you're aligning your feet. Then, put a club across your shoulders.

Lee Trevino has had a long, successful career aligning his body well left of his intended target and hitting push fades.

The clubface points at the target and the player's body lines (the shoulders, knees, hips, forearms, and feet) are all parallel to the target line. However, many successful players do not play from this model alignment. Lee Trevino and Fred Couples play by aligning considerably to the left and hitting push fades. Arnold Palmer and current tour players Jasper Parnevik and Rocco Mediate align to the right of their intended target and hit shots that are pulled or pull-hooked to the target. So did the late Sam Snead. Therefore, perhaps it's not necessary to set up with the model alignment.

The next time you're on the range, check your alignment by picking a target that is either on the left or the right side of the range and set up to the ball. Then, put a club along your feet and another club to where your clubface is aiming. You can also put a club across your shoulders and your hips to get an idea of how the rest of your body is aligned. It's helpful and more accurate if you can have someone else do all this for you while you're in your setup position. It's important to be aware of your body lines, where your shoulders, hips, and forearms are relative to where you are aligned. For example, when golfers have their shoulders and forearms open, facing to the left, the position tends to cause the golf club to move in that direction, thereby encouraging an outside-in clubhead path.

Now take a few steps back from the ball and look at where the clubs on the ground are pointing. This will give you a better idea of where your feet and clubface are aligned. Keep in mind that a player may have his or her clubface and body aligned parallel to the target line, but may prefer a foot line slightly to the left or right of these lines. Using this style of stance is acceptable and should be taken into account when checking and monitoring your alignment. For example, a closed stance can influence path and may encourage more of an inside-out path, while an open stance may encourage more of an outside-in path.

Try the above exercise a few times, using different targets on the range. Then, set the clubs up so that they are parallel to your target

---

Left: When the shoulders and forearms are open, aligned to the left, it can encourage an outside-in clubhead path. **Right:** *A stance alignment that is closed and aligned to the right can encourage an inside-in clubhead path.*

line, like the model. When you set up to the ball and look toward the target, if you had been aligning to the right, you'll now feel like you're aiming to the left. The distance to the left that you feel is an indicator of the amount to the right that you normally align yourself and have become comfortable with. If an alignment adjustment is needed, it is only through experience and practice that your eyes will readjust and get comfortable with a new alignment.

As I said earlier, most right-handed golfers align to the right of their target. The important point here is that most golfers aim at a target but align themselves to a different one. It helps to know where you are aligning yourself relative to your target so that you can more accurately read your ball flight and thereby make more effective swing changes. For example, let's assume that, like most golfers, you align yourself right of your target. How are you going to get the ball to the target? Which way will your path be? Out of necessity, you will swing from outside in and hit a pull or maybe a pull slice. If you hook the ball, you will find a way to compensate by closing the face, thereby curving the ball back to the target. No matter what your predominant ball flight is, your subconscious will always try to swing the club in a manner that will get the ball to go to your intended target. This is why it's important to understand where you are aligned relative to your intended target. Say you are working on straightening your slice and figure out how you need to change your path and your clubface in order to hit the ball straighter. You head out to the range to work on your new changes. That's great, but your feedback may become confusing. Remember the baseball diamond illustration used in Chapter 4; if your target is center field and you're aligned to right-center field, you don't want the model swing path and clubface alignment that produces straight shots, because the ball will go to right-center field every time. Your swing is shaped by your alignment. Or you could probably make the case that your alignment is shaped by your swing. Either way you look at it, one will affect the other, but the improvement process will be accelerated if you understand this relationship. Sometimes you'll need to change both your alignment and the movement of the club to achieve a compatible combination. However, I must emphasize that your alignment does not have to be perfect or exactly like the model. As I mentioned, many great players

The spot-aligning method requires an intermediary target—usually a piece of grass or any other tiny spot that catches the golfer's attention--directly between the ball and the actual target and generally within a few feet of the ball (above). Then, the player simply aligns himself or herself to that spot (below).

have had very successful careers aligning left or right of the target. But, whichever way you align, your alignment must be consistent in order for your golf swing to work well consistently.

Here are two different methods to improve and/or make your alignment more consistent. The first is spot-aligning. This method requires an intermediary target—usually a piece of grass or other tiny spot that catches the golfer's attention—directly between the ball and the actual target and within a few feet of the ball. Then, the player simply aligns himself or herself to that spot. The theory of this method is that it's much easier to align yourself to something two feet in front of you than to a target 200 yards away. This method works for a lot of players, but not for all. I personally can't use this method. I'll pick a spot looking from behind the ball and toward the target. Then, when I set up to the ball, I can't find the spot I picked out. This method just doesn't work for me. If you find this to be the case with you, here's the method that others, including myself, employ. Approach the ball from behind and set the clubhead down. Before taking your stance, try to align the clubface to the target, and then either align your body to the clubface, or, as I prefer, continue staring at the target as you take your setup with your body and feet. Then, when you look down at the ball, make any slight adjustments with your feet or body, if necessary.

Keep in mind that you have to practice alignment and monitor it to be more consistent and to get comfortable with any changes in your alignment. I don't believe that anyone ever masters alignment; it's something you'll always need to keep an eye on because you will always tend to direct your body to where you're comfortable. In the end, if you find that you're successful with aligning yourself a little to the right and hitting straight pulls, or aiming left and hitting straight pushes, or either of these flights with a controllable curvature, and can do it with a predictability you're satisfied with, don't fight it; just go ahead and employ it. *How a player aligns himself or herself is negotiable.*

Negotiable Element—GRIP

Your hands are the only things that are attached to the club, which is why your grip is one of the most important elements. The standard suggestion is to point the "Vs" (the

Fred Couples employs a closed-face grip, whereas Charles Howell utilizes one that is much more open-faced.

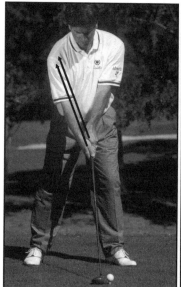

The three grip positions: closed-face (strong), open-face (weak), and neutral, which lies in between.

lines created by the thumbs when they are against the hands) to the right shoulder, or that you should see two knuckles on your left hand when you look down. Should that apply to everyone? Certainly not. Although the grip is one of the most important fundamentals because it influences face angle, there is much room for negotiability with it. A player's grip is very individual and the standard suggestions from sources in the golf community can be used as reference points, but not as solutions for all golfers. If you look at tour players, you'll see a considerable difference from player to player with regard to their hand positions. The two basic positions that represent both sides of the spectrum are a strong or closed-face position and a weak or open-face one. A neutral grip could be defined as something right in the middle of the two. The lines created by the thumbs and hands, and where they point relative to the right shoulder, are generally used as reference points. The more you rotate your hands in a direction, the more the clubface will be affected. When you grip the club, a counterclockwise rotation, from a player's perspective, causes the clubface to be more open at impact, while a clockwise rotation closes the face.

Sometimes golfers get confused with the grip and its impact on the clubface. One time I had a golfer with a 12 handicap say that he was really struggling. He said he normally hit his

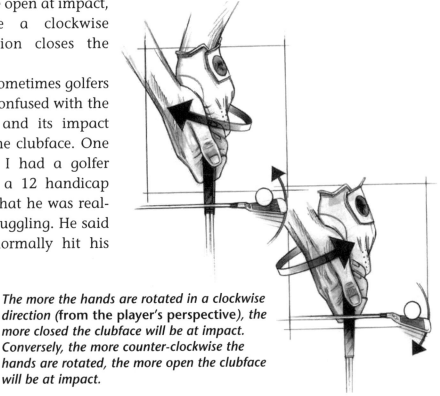

The more the hands are rotated in a clockwise direction (from the player's perspective), the more closed the clubface will be at impact. Conversely, the more counter-clockwise the hands are rotated, the more open the clubface will be at impact.

five iron about 170 yards. Watching him hit a few, I saw that he was hitting it high, to the right, and about 80 yards on a fly. When I asked him what he was working on, he told me his grip. The problem was that he thought he should be turning his hands one way, which was the exact opposite of what he needed to do. He thought that turning his hands more to the left, which is a more open-face position, would stop the high ball flight that was traveling a much shorter distance than normal. He kept rotating his hands to the point where the club-face was so open at impact that he effectively turned the loft of a five iron at impact into that of a sand wedge, which explains why he was only hitting the five iron about 80 yards.

Three types of grips are defined by how the fingers are placed on the club: interlocking, overlapping, and the ten-finger grip. All of these are acceptable styles. I encourage you to experiment with all three of them. Some grips are more comfortable than others, depending on hand and finger size as well as hand strength. Personally, I use the overlap grip, or what is sometimes referred to as the Vardon grip, named after the famous player Harry Vardon. I use it mostly because it's what my father taught me when I first started playing and it was the grip of choice at that time. Jim Furyk uses a version of the overlap grip, but he overlaps both his pinky finger and his ring finger. I've

The three most common grip types. The overlap or Vardon grip (left), the interlock grip (center), and the ten-finger or what is sometimes called the baseball grip (right).

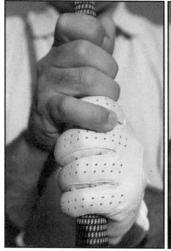 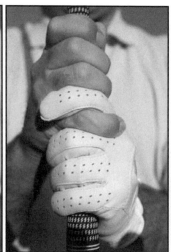 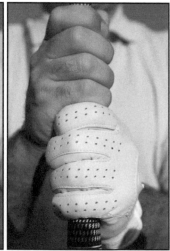

seen players do very well with the ten-finger grip, sometimes referred to as the "baseball' grip. This grip is the outcast in the golf community, but in my opinion there is nothing wrong with it. I think more golfers might be using it today, but generation after generation has been told that it is ineffective and incorrect to grip a club in this manner. A friend of mine, Dave Schepperle, a former PGA Professional, has two daughters, Candace and Abigale, who are excellent golfers and play on the University of Auburn golf team. Both are nationally ranked women amateurs. Candace, presently ranked among the top ten in the nation, employs the ten-finger grip. When I asked Dave about her using that grip, his response was simple: "It works for her."

Earlier, in the chapter on form and function, you saw that young Reece used a left-hand low grip, and although rare, mostly because it is considered incorrect, there are other players that have successfully employed this grip, as well.

Regardless of which grip you choose, I suggest keeping both hands close together and holding the club more in the fingers than the palms. The original design of the golf club required players to grip it in the palms. The PGA Teaching Manual, published in 1990, states "Grasping the club in the palms was a necessity from 1850 to1900 since the grips were 'built up' to cushion the shock from the gutta-percha ball." Nowadays, the golf club is thin by comparison to the original design; thus, to maintain control of the club throughout the swing, it is necessary to hold the club more in the fingers. With the left hand, the club is held diagonally, from the second knuckle of the pointer finger to a point where the butt of the club is in the palm, just below the pinky finger. With the right hand, the club is held between the first and second knuckles of the fingers.

If you wear a glove and wear out the heel of it, you are holding the club, with your left hand, too much in the palm. This causes the grip to move in the hand during the swing, creating friction and causing the glove to wear out on this spot. You need to move the placement of the grip of the club more into your fingers. Years ago, I went through dozens of gloves because of this, and I know golfers who even buy thicker gloves or the ones that have extra padding in the palm. Because the club is moving in the hand during the swing, it is possible the movement could cause the face angle to change, thereby

With the left hand the club is held diagonally, from the second knuckle of the pointer finger to a point where the butt of the club is in the palm, just below the pinky finger.

With the right hand, the club is held between the first and second knuckles of the fingers.

If you wear a glove and wear out the heel of it, you are holding the club, with your left hand, too much in the palm. You need to move the placement of the grip of the club more into your fingers.

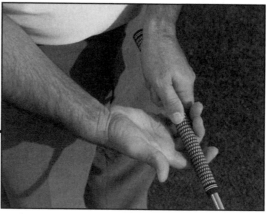

impacting the direction of the shot. In addition, when the club is held too much in the palm, it requires more muscle tension and pressure to control the golf club when it's being swung.

The amount of tension in your hands is important. Many will say that you should hold the club gently, as if you were holding a bird and you didn't want it to fly away. But when was the last time you held a bird in a way that it couldn't get away? And how big was the bird? Was it a canary or a bald eagle? Even if we all did hold the same bird, each of our experiences with how much pressure needed to be applied would be different. Obviously this idea is to encourage golfers to hold the club lightly and not strangle it with unnecessary tension in the

To better experience effective grip pressure, have someone stand opposite of you, and move the club while you try to maintain control and keep your arms and wrists relaxed.

hands. But what does that mean? And how can we determine this? One way to help feel how much tension is needed to hold the club is to have someone stand opposite of you and move your club randomly around in circles, up and down, and tug on the club trying to pull it out of your hands. Tell the other person not to get carried away; it's not a game of tug-of-war. The idea is to try maintaining enough pressure with your hands to control the club, but not so much that your arms and wrists cannot move freely. This exercise will help you experience how firm your grip needs to be to maintain control of the club and still allow your wrist and arms to be relaxed enough to function more effectively.

Some golfers hold the club with too little tension, or pressure, at the start of the swing and then have to tighten up somewhere in the swing. It's helpful to maintain the same grip pressure throughout the swing. The worn part of the glove mentioned earlier can also be evidence that a golfer is changing grip pressure, with the left hand opening and closing at points during the swing, causing friction. The most commonly accepted pressure points, where a little additional pressure could be applied, are the last three fingers of the left hand, the two middle fingers of the right, and the right palm pushing down on the left thumb. These are fine as a guideline, but can sometimes lead to more pressure than necessary. When you do the exercise above, you'll naturally feel where you need to apply pressure. The pressure between the pointer fingers and the thumbs of both hands is often overlooked.

If you make an "okay sign" and squeeze the pointer finger and thumb tightly together, you won't be able to shake your wrist. When you release the tension, you will be able to.

Make an "okay" sign with your right hand and very firmly squeeze the pointer finger and the thumb together. While doing this, try to shake your hand from the wrist, as you might do if your hand "fell asleep." What you'll notice is that unless you release the pressure between your fingers, you will not be able to shake your hand. This is evidence that if you squeeze these two fingers together, with either hand, it will inhibit your ability to allow your wrists to remain flexible throughout the swing. I really like this idea; "Firm grip, relaxed wrists," which is how teaching professional Jim Petaglia is quoted in Mike Hebron's book, *Golf Swing Secrets...and Lies: Six Timeless Lessons*.

Many times I suggest a grip adjustment and place the golfer's hands on the club, then the golfer won't let go of the club between shots. Don't take the grip once and continue to rake balls over without letting go in fear that you'll lose your "new" grip. Part of learning a new grip is learning the routine of taking the new grip each time you place your hands on the club. Using a mirror can be very helpful when learning a new grip. Once you determine and learn the most effective grip for your full swing, I suggest you use it for chipping and pitching the ball. Some advocate using a different grip (more open-face) for the short game. This is negotiable and if it works for you, that's fine. I personally use the same grip throughout my game, except when putting.

In Chapter 4, you learned that the natural movement of the club-face is inside-square-inside. Although it is the natural rotation of the clubface, the amount of face rotation needed depends on the positions of your hands on the club; some players need more and others need less face rotation. Players with more open-face grips tend to rotate the clubface more; players with closed-face grips tend to rotate it less. Also keep in mind that when a grip adjustment and/or a path adjustment is made, how you rotate the clubface may have been conditioned by the way you were swinging the club. Golfers who slice the ball are conditioned to holding the face open through impact, and do so out of necessity so that they can get the ball curving back to the target. Hookers do the opposite. You may need to do some experimenting with either inhibiting or encouraging face rotation, depending on what you were doing and what you need to do after you make changes.

I remember one lesson I had with David Glenz. I asked his opinion about my recent grip change, which had my hands in a very closed-face position. He said it was fine because when I addressed the ball, the clubface was a little open. It didn't look open to me, but it was and he showed me why. The grip was very comfortable for me and he said I really didn't have to change it since at address I set up with the face slightly open the same amount, and thus my grip was offsetting the open clubface. Since then, I have tried to square off my face angle at address and modify my grip, but I continue to go back to what's comfortable, and as long as I do it consistently, it's functional. It's what works for me. *How a player grips the club is negotiable.*

Negotiable Element—BALL POSITION

A   B

Two ball positions are shown in the photo here.

If you were hitting a five iron, which one would you prefer, "A" or "B"? Your preference can tell you a lot about your path without seeing the ball flight. Two basic schools of thought on ball position exist, and the jury is still out on these two philosophies. The first is called a static-ball position, where the ball is played under the left armpit, or some say inside the left heel, regardless of the club being used. The second, which has become the more accepted method, is a variable-ball position, where the driver is played just inside the left heel and

The guidelines for the variable ball position method: The ball just inside the left heel with the driver (left), a little farther back in the stance with the mid-irons (center), and just forward of the middle of the stance with a wedge.

When viewed together, the distance apart in each of the ball positions doesn't vary that much.

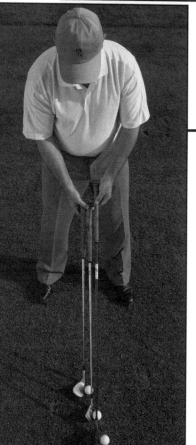

a sand wedge is played just forward of the center of the stance. The distance that the ball moves from driver to wedge is not as great as most golfers think. Of course, these positions are for standard shots from level lies. Many times the ball position needs to be changed based on other factors, such as lie (in the rough), slope (ball above your feet), or the need to hit the ball higher or lower. My experience is that ball position is a little different for everyone, but I prefer and suggest that you use the variable-ball position as a guideline. I say guideline because even within the parameters of the variable-ball position, a player has to move the ball more forward or back in the stance, depending on his or her swing path. I've

A ball played farther back in the stance encourages an inside-out clubhead path. Conversely, a ball played more forward in the stance will encourage an outside-in swing path.

seen one player be success-ful with a ball position with a driver that is a ball's width inside the left heel, and another player who plays the driver off his left instep.

Earlier I mentioned that you can tell a lot about your path by observ-ing which of the two ball positions, either back or forward in the stance, you prefer. A ball played farther back in the stance encourages an inside approach and is preferred by those that hook the ball. More forward in the stance encourages an outside approach and is preferred by golfers who slice the ball. If you slice the ball, you may have a tendency to play the ball very forward in your stance, and if you don't change the position, that same ball position will continue to encourage the outside-in path that you are trying to change. The forward-ball position requires an outside-in path. I, personally, have to carefully monitor my ball position. Since my tendency is to swing the club excessively from the inside, it does-n't take long for my ball position to start creeping back in my stance to match my swing path, which unfortunately creates the push and hook that I fight. *Because effective ball positions can vary from player to player, ball position is negotiable.*

Remember, when you work on these elements to improve your ball flight, many times you will need to adjust more than one element to find the compatible arrangement that will work for you. This chapter focused on the pre-swing elements that most influence direction. However, many golfers will also pick up distance as a result of changing a pre-swing element because it can improve the relationship of the clubface and path of the clubhead without any speed being added. Work on direction and control before focusing on speed and distance.

CHAPTER 7

The Elements of Speed

T he emphasis in the last couple of chapters was on making sure that you hit the ball straight before you focus on hitting it farther. As the saying goes, "There are plenty of long-hitters in the woods." In those chapters, I discussed swing plane, the right side of the body, the pre-swing elements, and how they all impact the movement of the golf club. All these factors have a primary influence on direction, with a secondary influence on distance. In this chapter, I focus on the elements of the body that directly influence how fast your golf club travels—the speed of which influences the distance the ball will travel—with a secondary influence on direction.

In the last chapter, we looked at the swing from mainly the perspective of behind a golfer; now look at it from a face-on perspective. The golf swing from start to finish looks like the photo sequence on pages 112-113.

Effective golf swings are unique from player to player and have been so since the birth of the game. However, regardless of the individual stylistic variations of a player swinging the club, we can say five basic things about the body and arms and their role in creating speed in the golf swing: (See photo sequence on pages 112-113)

1. The body pivots (turns, rotates) back on the backswing and forward to the finish position. (No. 1-8)
2. The arms and wrists create angles on the backswing. (No. 2, 3)
3. The angles are maintained in the downswing. (No. 4, 5)
4. The angles are expanded through impact. (No. 6)
5. Angles are recreated after impact and into the finish. (No. 7, 8)

Bobby Jones Ben Hogan Arnold Palmer Jack Nicklaus

1. *The body pivots (turns, rotates) back on the backswing and forward to the finish position. (1-8)*
2. *The arms and wrists create angles on the backswing. (2, 3)*

In essence, the body is our engine, and that engine needs to move the golf club. If the club is used effectively, the faster it moves, the more energy is transferred to the ball, and the farther distance the ball travels. To maximize speed, minimize effort, and gain distance, we need to use both our body and arms. Similar basic movements can be

In many motions, such as hitting a baseball, playing tennis, and swinging an axe, the body rotates, the arms and wrists create angles, and then those angles expand through impact.

Tom Watson   Nick Faldo   Greg Norman   Tiger Woods

3. The angles are maintained in the downswing. (4, 5)
4. The angles are expanded through impact. (6)
5. Angles are recreated after impact and into the finish. (7, 8)

observed in motions, such as hitting a baseball, playing tennis, and swinging an axe. In all of these motions, just as in golf, the body is rotating, the arms and wrists are creating angles, and then those angles are expanding through impact.

First, look at the core movement of the body. I use the term "pivot" as opposed to "turn" to describe the rotation of the body in the golf swing. You are likely to encounter many tips on how to pivot in the backswing, such as "Don't sway," "Keep your head still," and "Take a

full shoulder turn." These tips only confuse golfers because they lead golfers to believe that they should pivot around the spine. Golfers who turn around their spines or keep their heads still while making their backswing do not allow for the pivot to be made from the

Focusing only on the hips, the golfer pivots into the right hip on the backswing (1), transitions out of it and into a "neutral" position on the downswing (2), then continues to pivot completely into the left hip socket (3).

hip sockets, which, from a design standpoint of the human body, is a more effective way to pivot. The shoulders do turn around the spine in the swing, but I believe it may be more useful for golfers to think about their hip sockets as pivot points. Focusing only on the hips, the golfer pivots into the right hip on the backswing, transitions out of it and into a "neutral" position on the downswing, then continues to pivot completely into the left hip socket.

Negotiable Element—LATERAL BACKSWING MOVEMENT

In the 1980s, Curtis Strange's golf swing brought him some attention because he was making a very pronounced movement into his right side, allowing his spine to move back away

Above: *Place a piece of tape on a full-length mirror to use as a point of reference for your head. Then, without a club, make a backswing pivot, rotating your upper body into your right hip socket.* **Below:** *Your head should move slightly to the right of the tape line.*

Right: *A reverse pivot occurs when the weight moves toward the front foot on the backswing, and then, for many players, reverses and moves to the back foot on the downswing* (below).

from the ball and positioning much of his weight onto his right foot at the top of the backswing. Some referred to it as a sway. It was an exaggerated movement compared to other players, a move that he learned from his instructor, Jimmy Ballard. Now the movement is considered very acceptable and is taught by many instructors. Allowing the head to "float" or "drift" to the right is how it is now described. Using a mirror, you can experience a backswing pivot that utilizes the right hip socket and allows for some movement to the right. Place a piece of tape on the mirror to use as a point of reference for your head. Without a club, make a backswing pivot, rotating your shoulders and feeling your upper body pivot weight into your right hip socket. You'll notice that your head moves slightly to your right when you do this and you feel more pressure in your right foot. A reverse pivot occurs when the weight moves toward the front foot on the backswing, and then, for many players, reverses and moves to the back foot on the downswing. The golf club is going back away from the target on the backswing as the body is going toward the target. Then, on the downswing, the golf club is moving down and forward toward the target while the body is moving backward, away from it. This is obviously not a very natural move. If you make a backswing that utilizes your right hip and allows the spine and head to "drift" back a little in the backswing, the reverse pivot can't happen. However, that being said, the amount of lateral movement that the upper body moves to the right in the backswing is not an absolute. If you examine swings of tour players past and present, you can see a difference in the permissible amount of lateral motion a player

Backswing lateral motion is negotiable. Some players, like Colin Montgomerie, have been successful with little movement. Others, like Curtis Strange, have a pronounced movement to the right.

employs in his or her backswing. Players have been successful with little movement or a pronounced movement to the right, or any amount in between. Many modern-day players make a pronounced move to the right; however, other players, such as José María Olazábal, Colin Montgomerie, and David Duval don't move much at all. In fact, some consider these players to have a reverse pivot, as they stay centered at the top of their backswing with a minimal, if any, amount of movement to the right. However, they stay centered on their downswing and finish on their left side. You'll need to experiment with how much lateral movement on the backswing works best for you. *The amount the player moves laterally in the backswing is negotiable.*

The Transition

Once a player has completed the backswing, we come to the next phase, another commonly talked about area of the swing: the transition. This is the transitional movement from the top of the backswing into the downswing. Some golfers and instructors use the idea of "shifting" the weight from the right foot to the left foot to initiate the transition into the downswing. This idea is somewhat intuitive because it's common knowledge that the weight is a little on the right side at the top of the backswing and then nearly all of the weight is on the left foot at the finish. But weight-shifting can lead to further problems. Instead of referring to weight, let's call it pressure. On the backswing, we can feel more pressure in our right foot, but on the downswing, the pressure doesn't shift quickly over to the left side. Actually, the force and the pressure move down into the ground and

When working on your transition from backswing to downswing (1), feel the right shoulder going down, your arms and right elbow moving down in front of your body, and pressure going down into both feet (2). When the right shoulder goes down on the downswing, the spine tilts backward, away from the target, putting the head behind the ball at impact (3).

can be felt in both feet before moving completely over to the left side. It's a gradual movement in which the force moves down. The idea that the weight moves laterally, or from side to side, can be dangerous and ineffective. We need the ground for leverage, something to push against. Simple tests have been done with golfers standing on two bathroom scales; on the downswing their weight on the scales reads higher than the golfer's actual weight because force in the transition is moving downward. If we were floating in outer space, we couldn't generate the same amount of club speed because we wouldn't be able to use our bodies in the same way without having the ground for leverage.

In the last chapter, I discussed the right shoulder and its use to direct the line and path of the club on the downswing. When working on your transition from backswing to downswing, you may find it helpful to simultane-

Impact. Right shoulder down, spine tilting backward, head behind the ball.

ously feel the right shoulder going down, your arms and right elbow moving down in front of your body, and pressure going down into both feet. Notice how everything in the transition is going down, not

forward. This simple move can improve several elements all at the same time. Also, when the right shoulder goes down on the downswing, the spine tilts backward, away from the target, which puts the head behind the ball at impact; a common denominator in nearly all sound swings. Then, the rotation of the body continues and moves nearly all the pressure into the left foot at the finish position.

The Power Illusion

But which part of the body, when it's rotating, does the power in the golf swing come from? Many focus on the legs and hips, but the evidence shows otherwise. While the legs may play a small role, I believe most players would benefit from the idea that the legs play a supporting, as opposed to an active, role on the downswing. You can experience this by hitting balls with your feet very close together. You'll probably feel your upper body doing the work and your legs more or less responding to that movement. In addition, you'll notice that you can hit the ball pretty close to the normal distance you would with your feet together as when they're apart. The fact of the matter is that the legs don't play the power role that golfers believe they do. Some trick shot artists can hit the ball a high percentage of their normal distance while sitting in a chair, on their knees, or standing on one foot, again proving that the legs are not the major

Hitting balls with the feet very close together allows a golfer to experience the inactive role the lower body plays in the golf swing.

PGA Professional Ben Witter can hit balls over 300 yards while standing on a large exercise ball.

power supply in the golf swing. To confirm these ideas, I e-mailed Ben Witter, a fellow PGA Professional who is also a well-respected trick shot artist. Ben knows a little about power; he was a two-time NCAA long drive champion and has the ability to hit a driver 300 yards while standing on a large exercise ball. I told him about my book and my ideas on the role of the legs in the golf swing. Ben wrote back to me:

> Joe,
> I have a very interesting story to tell you about your work. I was doing a trick shot performance for the Buick Invitational where I stand on the (exercise) ball and hit a shot out of midair. Several PGA Tour pros were in attendance. Just prior to my show, these tour professionals performed a clinic, during which they told the audience that the hips and legs were the most important elements of the swing.
> After I did my shots, several people in the audience asked the pros "If the legs and hips are the most important elements of the swing, then how can this guy hit a ball 300 yards while standing on the ball?" There were no answers from the pros that were still there.
> The bottom line...the CORE and HANDS are what generate compression power in the golf swing. The legs and hips are simply the foundation from which to apply this compression power.
> If you would like to chat more, please give me a call sometime.
> Ben

I called him, we had a chuckle about the story, and I asked if he hits the ball 300 yards while standing on the ball and how far he hits the ball while standing on the ground. He told me about 340-350, proving that more than 85% of his power while standing on the ball comes from his upper torso and his arms, since when standing on the ball his lower body needs to stay relatively still in order to create a foundation that will allow him to keep his balance.

Yet many believe that the hips are a great source of power. One reason for this belief is that if you look at the swings of top players, it seems that the hips move faster than the shoulders do. This, however, is just an illusion. The hips are more "open" at impact, facing the target, and this is what leads the eyes to believe that the hips move faster

On the backswing, the shoulders rotate about 90 degrees and the hips about 45 degrees (left). *At impact, the shoulders have moved 90 degrees, basically back to their original position at address, while the hips have moved 90 degrees to a position that is 45 degrees open* (right). *The shoulders and hips have moved at a similar rate of rotation.*

than the shoulders. If we look at the downswing more closely, we can see that. In the model backswing, the shoulders move about 90 degrees and the hips about 45 degrees. At impact, the shoulders have moved 90 degrees, basically back to their original position at address. The hips are now 45 degrees open, facing toward the target; thus, they have also moved 90 degrees, from 45 degrees in the backswing to being open 45 degrees at impact. They have basically moved the same amount (90 degrees) on the downswing. In essence, the hips and shoulders have moved at the same rate of rotation. This also illustrates how and why impact and address positions are not the same. If you want to get technical, remember that earlier I illustrated why longer clubs naturally move faster than shorter ones and how the horses on the outside of the merry-go-round, because they are travel-

ing on a bigger circle, are moving faster than the horses on the inside, on the smaller circle. If you looked at a golfer's hips and shoulders from above, you would see that during the swing they create two circles. For most individuals, the shoulders are wider than the hips. When both are rotating in a circular motion at the same rate, the shoulders, which have a wider diameter, create a bigger circle that moves faster than that of the hips, which create a smaller circle.

Impact positions are quite different from address positions.

The length of a golfer's back-swing is negotiable and is dictated in part by his or her flexibility. Some golfers are better off with a longer back-swing, while others with a shorter one.

Negotiable Element— AMOUNT OF PIVOT

The amount you are able to pivot depends on your personal flexibility in both your upper body and your hips. Do not be concerned if the amount your shoulders turn on the backswing is less than the model 90 degrees. Going past the point your flexibility and physical attributes allow will cause more problems than benefits. Forget the idea that you have to take a really big backswing or get the club to a parallel position at the top to hit the ball correctly. The fact that we don't use a full backswing when we chip or pitch the ball is evidence that the length of the backswing is not mandatory in order to effectively swing the club.

Other advice, such as "Wind up on the backswing," or "Turn the shoulders but restrict the hips," tries

John Daly came on the scene in the '90s with an unorthodox long back-swing. Champions Tour player Allen Doyle employs a very short backswing (yes, this is the TOP of his backswing!).

to convince golfers that by doing this they are winding up like a rubber band, storing energy so that it can be released on the downswing. However, our muscles are not rubber bands. They do not stretch and then release power in this manner. These notions can also lead to over-rotation of the shoulders, a pivot that is unnecessarily restricted, and a reverse pivot, all of which can have a negative effect and destroy a good backswing pivot. Taking a backswing pivot as far back as possible may create an initial "stretch reflex," a movement that causes the body to start to move in the other direction because the golfer can't hold that position. Such a movement can be somewhat helpful in making a smooth transition from backswing to downswing, but the idea of really trying to increase your backswing should be approached with caution. *The length of the backswing, as well as the amount the hips move versus the shoulders, is negotiable.*

Negotiable Element—STANCE

The stance a golfer takes is negotiable and is a player preference. It's a pre-swing element but has a primary influence on how much a player can pivot, which is why I include it here. Generally, you should stand wider with the long clubs and narrower with the shorter ones. The model stance is with the distance between inside of your feet just wider than shoulders' width for the driver, getting progressively narrower, to just inside the shoulder line, for the wedges. The model works well as a starting point, but keep in mind that it is perfectly fine to vary from it. The most important thing is for your stance to be comfortable and allow you to stay balanced. Be aware that very narrow stances may make it more difficult to maintain

Stance width is variable and negotiable. The model stance is with the distance between the inside of your feet just wider than shoulders' width for the driver (left), getting progressively narrower, to just inside the shoulder line, for the wedges (right).

balance. Conversely, very wide stances can restrict your ability and the amount you can rotate and pivot your body on the backswing. *The width of a golfer's stance is negotiable.*

Negotiable Element—THE HEAD AND THE EYES

My all-time least favorite and most damaging tips that golfers encounter are to "Keep your head down" and/or "Keep your eyes on the ball." These are probably the two oldest and most shared tips that exist, and they probably started because many times beginners completely miss the ball. Other common misses for even more experienced players are the topped shot, where the ball doesn't get in the air, or the thin or bladed shot, where the club strikes the equator of the ball and flies on a low line drive trajectory. Because all of these shots have the club moving too high off the ground, the first conclusion drawn is that the person is lifting up, thereby causing the club to travel too high in relation to the ground. The supposed remedy for this is to keep the head down or for the golfer to keep his or her eyes on the ball. But the fact of the matter is that although the lifting of the body can be the cause of these shots, many times it is not. And even when it is, it's not caused by the head moving. We don't lead our body around by our heads.

The idea of a player keeping his or her head down is nothing short of horrible and causes more damage than good. The fear of lifting or not moving the head in the backswing can cause the reverse pivot,

Keeping the head down in the backswing blocks the shoulder on the backswing (left) *and inhibits the backswing pivot. On the downswing, it inhibits a player's ability to continue rotation and motion through impact and into the finish* (right).

Annika Sorenstam does not look at the ball at impact; rather, her eyes and head both rotate with her body through impact.

block a player's shoulder on the backswing, and thus inhibit the backswing pivot. A result of this thinking also leads to one of the most damaging things on the downswing: inhibiting a player's ability to continue rotation and motion through impact and into the finish. When a player tries to keep his or her head down, the body rotation comes to a halt. This is why some golfers have trouble coming to a complete finish position. And as far as keeping the eyes on the ball is concerned, blind golfers can play some pretty good golf. Bob Rotella, the world-renowned sports psychologist, tells the story in his book, *Life Is Not a Game of Perfect*, of a golfer who had an accident and lost his eyesight. He was determined to still play and, with the help of a personal coach who acted as his eyes, relearned the game. In 1980, at the Braille Tournament at Mission Hills in Palm Springs, he shot, from the middle tees, consecutive rounds of 75, 74, 79, and 75.

The reality is that golfers don't miss the ball because they take their eyes off it. The head and eyes should naturally move with the body and the golf club. Several professional golfers, including Annika Sorenstam, David Duval, and Joe Durant, all play golf with their eyes actually looking toward the target at impact. And although I certainly cannot put myself in their class, I also play golf with my head rotating and my eyes looking toward the target at impact. I also got into the habit of keeping my head down too long, which inhibited my rotation through impact and into the finish. A few years ago I started working on my rotation and as a by-product my head and eyes started rotating forward just before impact. I actually found it to be very natural and it allowed my downswing rotation to be much freer and less inhibited. I'm not suggesting that you do this, but rather try to let your head and eyes naturally follow the ball. This will enable your body rotation to become faster and smoother, and you will experience more freedom. *How a player uses his or her head and eyes in the golf swing is negotiable.*

THE WRISTS AND ARMS

Next, let's turn to the wrist and arms and see how they move in the golf swing. At the start of this chapter I illustrated how in the golf swing the arms and wrists create angles on the backswing, maintain them on the downswing, and release them through impact. These are common denominators in all effective swings, but there is some negotiability with how these actions are performed.

Negotiable Element—THE WRIST SET

Because you don't hit the ball with your backswing, it's another area where you can negotiate how things are done. Where and how these angles are created can vary greatly from player to player. The creation of these is referred to as hinging, cocking, or setting. When it happens is defined as early, mid, and late. An early set is when the wrist angles are created at the very start of the backswing and are completed when the hands are just past the right hip. Mid is a little later, and a late set happens as the club is approaching the top of the backswing. The "one-piece takeaway" and the late set were popular in years past and still are with some instructors. This takeaway theory maintains that the imaginary triangle formed by the arms and the shoulders should stay intact for most of the backswing, thereby causing the wrists to set after the left arm is at least past parallel to the ground. Players like Jack Nicklaus and Tiger Woods employ this type of takeaway and late wrist set. Some players actually increase the angle in their wrists on the downswing, a move that is referred to as downcocking. You can see this

Some players prefer to set the angles earlier in the backswing (left), whereas others prefer to set them later (right).

Below: *Some players, like Sergio Garcia, create an angle with their wrists on the backswing, then increase the amount of that angle on the downswing.*

The golf swing can start with the wrists in a pre-set position.

action in the swings of Ben Hogan and modern-day tour player Sergio Garcia.

Where the player sets his or her wrists is a personal preference. There is, however, definitely a trend to set them early in the backswing, the theory being that if you get it done earlier, less can go wrong later. There may be some truth to this but it's not mandatory, and the method is not for everyone. Just look at the tour players. Where they create the angles with their wrists varies from player to player. Actually, the golf swing could start with the wrists in a pre-set position. Recently, I saw a couple of PGA and LPGA players, Ryan Moore and Suzann Pettersen, on television and observed them employing this style with their backswings. This method would probably work just fine for a lot of golfers, but golfers are traditionalists by nature and can be reluctant to differ from the norm. If a golfer came to see me and was already doing this, I would leave that part of the swing alone, provided it wasn't causing any other negative effects. Personally, I don't think about when and where I set my wrists. I let my wrists naturally create angles through momentum. In other words, I keep my wrists relaxed and the weight and momentum of the club creates the angles. Experiment with different methods and see what works best for you. *Where, when, and how a player sets his or her wrists in the backswing is negotiable.*

If the left arm is bending excessively, it's because the right arm is folding past 90 degrees.

Negotiable Element—LEFT ARM BEND

The most popular idea for the left arm is not to allow it to bend throughout the swing, especially during the backswing and at the top of the swing. In fact, if you viewed videos of world-class players, you would see that most of them have their left arms relatively straight throughout the backswing. The left arm can maintain the radius in the circular motion that the arms make in the golf swing, but it's the right arm that is actually doing the work to keep the left arm fairly straight. If the left arm is bending excessively, it's because the right arm is folding past 90 degrees. When the right arm maintains a 90-degree angle, the left arm stays fairly straight. Focusing on keeping the left arm straight by utilizing the left arm alone, however, most likely will cause excessive tension in the arms, and tension in the arms kills speed. If the left arm bends a little, it's not necessarily bad. In fact, since it is increasing the angles of the arms, it can actually produce more speed. However, creating too much angle can cause control to suffer. A 90-degree bend in the right arm and a slight flex in the left is a good rule of thumb. *The amount a player bends the left arm in the backswing is negotiable.*

When the right arm maintains a 90-degree angle, the left arm stays fairly straight.

MAINTAIN THE LAG

After you have worked on creating the angles on the backswing with the wrist set and arms, look at what to do with these angles. In a sound golf swing, those angles are maintained at the beginning of

Right: *Angles maintained on the downswing are a common denominator in all great swings, both past and present. Gene Sarazen (1935) and Tiger Woods.*

Below: *When the right arm straightens too early on the downswing (casting), the angles are straightened prematurely and much of the golf club's potential energy is lost.*

the downswing. In fact, maintaining these angles, or what is referred to as holding the angle or lag, is a common denominator in all world-class players' golf swings. This movement enables energy, or power, to be stored so that it can be released later in the downswing, closer to impact, thereby creating more clubhead speed. Let's rule out one thing from the start: the angles are not maintained through muscular tension in the wrists and arms. While it can be done in this manner, it creates tension in the arms and makes it very difficult to time the release of the angles at impact. Unfortunately, many golfers employ this method in an effort to not "cast" the club from the top. Casting basically means the angles in the wrists are released, or expanded, too early in the downswing. However, it's not the right wrist that's the culprit as most believe; it's

The angles in the wrists and right arm are still maintained very late in the downswing.

From a player's perspective, it appears that it would be impossible to hit the ball if the angles are maintained this late in the downswing. This lag creates clubhead speed and power.

the right arm. I don't think I have ever seen a golfer who straightened his or her right arm early but maintained the angles in the wrists. The straightening of the right arm sets off a chain reaction that causes the wrists to lose their angles. I believe that one of the reasons golfers release the angles prematurely is that it is counterintuitive to maintain the angles. Whenever I physically put a golfer in a position that demonstrates what the club should look like on the downswing, with hands in front of the right hip and the angles still maintained, the player's instinct seems to indicate that the club will pass right over the ball and he or she will never be able to square the clubface. This is understandable, especially when viewed from the perspective of the player, but is where our instincts get in the way and our subconscious can cause us to release the angles early. This especially applies to golfers who slice the ball and fear hitting it to the right.

Poor posture can also contribute to an early release. When I discussed posture in the previous chapter, I talked about how the upper body spine angle is important to getting the right arm, with its angle maintained, in front of the right hip. Without adequate spine angle, the right arm has no room to get in front of the golfer's right hip; thus, the golfer may straighten the right arm early in an effort to get the arms in front of the body and hit the ball. Martin Hall saw this in my swing. In my backswing, I was losing my spine angle, or what Martin described as going "belly up," where my belt buckle was moving towards the ball in my backswing, causing me to lose my spine angle and thereby blocking the path for my arms on the downswing, necessitating releasing the angles of my arms and wrists too early. Once I learned to maintain my posture throughout my swing, my arms were able to find the room they need on the downswing, enabling me to properly maintain and release the angles of my arms and wrists.

Earlier I gave a suggestion on how to work on the transition, by having the arms and right elbow go down while feeling the pressure go into both feet. When you do this, focus on keeping the angles intact with the arms and wrists relaxed. Don't use excessive tension; it's not needed to maintain the angles.

THE MOMENT THAT COUNTS

Now comes the moment of truth: releasing the angles through impact. Expanding the angles through impact generates and maximizes speed and happens very late in the downswing, evident by the fact that the angles are still intact with the hands in front of the right hip, and then begin to straighten as the hands approach the ball. Note also how the handle of the club is slightly forward of the club-head at impact. This is important as the golf club is designed with the grip and shaft in front of the clubhead. Immediately after impact, all angles have been expanded, both arms are straight, and the left arm and clubshaft create a straight line. This is the point where both arms are straight and is what is referred to as the "follow-through" position. The term follow-through is many times used synonymously with the

The angles continue to straighten as the hands approach the impact zone (1). At impact, the hands and handle end of the club are still slightly forward of the clubhead (2). The follow-through position: all angles have been expanded, both arms are straight, and the left arm and clubshaft create a straight line (3).

Because of the difference in speed, the race car will catch up to the runner, even though the runner has the lead, just as the clubhead will catch up to the hands at impact.

term "finish," but I refer to the finish position as the end of the swing.

The image and idea of extending the arms through impact unfortunately can encourage a golfer to release the angles early on the downswing, which can lead to the casting motion. It helps to understand how these angles can expand when the hands are far in front of the clubhead on the downswing, and the club catches up to the hands to become in line with them at impact. The club moves very quickly as it approaches impact; to use approximate numbers, let's say the clubhead on the driver is moving at 100 miles per hour at impact, but the hands, which create a smaller arc, are moving only about 10 miles per hour (the body, which creates the smallest arc, is

The "swoosh" drill. Turn the club around and swing the grip end to improve the storing and release of energy through impact.

only rotating at about 4 miles per hour). It would be like watching a very short race between a race car and a runner. Imagine a runner, moving at 10 miles per hour, only a step away from the finish line, and the race car, moving 100 miles per hour, considerably farther away from it. Because of the difference in their speeds, they could cross the finish line at nearly the same time. In the golf swing, the hands win this race and beat the clubhead to the ball, as they are slightly more forward than the clubhead at impact. To experience the speed and acceleration of the club through impact, take your driver and turn it around as if you were going to hit the ball with the grip of the club. Swing the club and try to hear the "swoosh" sound after the point where the ball would be if you were to hit it. The later and louder the sound, the more power and speed has been maintained, and then released through impact. If you hear the sound early in the downswing, it means the angles were prematurely expanded and energy was lost, energy that won't get to the ball.

Negotiable Element—POWER SOURCE

I've talked about the body and how energy and speed are derived, which is a combination of the rotation of the body and the swinging of the arms. The ratios players use of these power sources, and how the angles are ultimately expanded, can be by two different methods: swinging and hitting. It helps to understand the difference between the two. The swinging style occurs when the pull of centrifugal force, through the rotation of the body, straightens the arms' and wrists' angles. This motion can be seen in other activities, such as a discus throw or a field goal kick in football.

The hitting method is different. The player physically, through muscular effort, straightens the right arm and wrist through impact. This same motion can be observed in other sports, such as a basketball free throw or the shot put. If you observe and study the different golf swings, this part of the swing looks very similar and it can be difficult to differentiate a hitting motion from a swinging motion. In the hitting motion, the right arm straightens and the expansion of the angles takes place very late in the downswing, just as it does with the swinging method. However, caution must be used when experimenting with this method. If the player expands the angle of the right arm too early, it will become a casting motion.

The discus throw and field goal kick are motions similar to the swinging method in golf.

The shot put and free throw are motions similar to the hitting method in golf.

You can experience the hitting and swinging methods with the "swoosh" exercise provided earlier. As you do this exercise, relax your arms and maintain the angles, allowing centrifugal force to pull your arms and wrists straight, thereby releasing the angles. Then, to experience the hitting motion, try straightening your right arm very late in the downswing to release the angles.

Top players in the world use both methods. Generally speaking, players who are faster and more flexible use a swinging motion, whereas players who are stronger and less flexible use a hitting motion. The reality is that no player exclusively uses one method or the other. Players are using a combination of both, but with varying degrees. *The power source a player chooses to use is negotiable.*

We've now explored how the body and the arms create the speed in the golf swing, but my observations and discussion have been mostly from a standpoint of breaking them down individually. Next, we need to look at putting them together as a unit and a complete motion.

The Elements of Time and Space

So far we have broken down and discussed many different elements and parts of the full swing. However, the golf swing is an entire motion that is a blending of these parts and takes place in time and in space. Many times you'll hear golfers say that they are trying to take the timing out of their swing. Really, though, it's impossible to take the timing out of your golf swing. The fact is that with the average player the club is moving up to 90 miles per hour with a driver, and at impact must strike the ball with the clubface precisely at the right moment and at the precise angles to make that little white object fly straight to its target. An error of a few degrees in the clubface angle is the difference between the middle of the fairway and a shot that goes in the rough. Timing has to be involved.

Rhythm and tempo are often used synonymously, but it's important to recognize their differences. Rhythm is the sequence of movements that takes place in the golf swing. When a player is said to have good rhythm, he or she has a fluid, harmonious sequencing of these movements. Timing is defined as properly timing the sequence of movements that takes place before impact to produce the desired results. Tempo is the amount of time that it takes from start to finish in the golf swing. Ideally, we want to effectively time the sequence of these movements in a repeatable amount of time on every swing.

Negotiable Element—TEMPO

You have an internal clock that beats with a tempo that is uniquely yours and is reflected in the pace of your golf swing. Some people walk, eat, and talk fast, while others perform these activities more slowly. In golf, trying to change to a tempo that is not natural for you can be disastrous. Watch tour players and you'll see some swing at a slower tempo, like Ernie Els, while others like Nick Price swing with a relatively quick tempo. However, they both look smooth doing it, it's just at a different pace. It's important to swing at your own unique, optimal tempo. This will help you swing with better rhythm and timing, translating into a more effective and powerful motion that, in turn, translates into better contact, increased distance, and improved direction control.

Many times you'll hear the phrase "Slow down your swing." This common suggestion is really just another one of those catchall remedies for every bad shot. For most golfers, the concept of slowing down their swing leads to the belief that their swing will be better. Psychologically, slowing down a swing can also be difficult and challenging, and somewhat counterintuitive, because we know we need to create speed on the downswing. When you try to generate speed from the top of the backswing, instinct can take over. After all, the club is traveling a short distance from the top to impact, starting at 0 and moving up to 100 miles per hour at impact in less than a half second. This can be especially counterintuitive with the driver, a club with which most golfers try to swing harder and faster to hit the longest drive possible. It becomes a case of the conscious and the subconscious fighting each other, which is why many times golfers struggle and complain that they can't slow down their swing. Slow is good if you want to hit the ball very short. I see this in many golfers' practice swings. They'll show me their practice swing with a driver and comment on how slow and effortless it looks and how they can't produce that same swing when the ball is there. Why would they want to? With that slow motion swing, the ball would go only about 50 yards.

An ear metronome, a device normally used by musicians, can be very helpful to golfers working on the tempo of their swing.

Working with a metronome can be very useful in helping you work on your own tempo for your golf swing. A metronome, a device normally used by musicians, especially drummers, emits an audible beep or click and can be set to a specific number of beats per minute. The beeps help musicians develop a better and more consistent sense of time. Using a metronome can help you in two ways. It can assist you in finding your own personal tempo from the start of your swing to impact. This is measured by a certain number of beats per minute. Once you find your natural tempo, you can practice working on your rhythm to that tempo. What's really interesting is that your tempo, from the start of your swing to impact, is the same for a three-foot putt as it is for a full swing with your driver. This seems impossible because the putterhead is only going back several inches and the driver is going back several feet, covering a much greater distance. Try this and you will be amazed at how they are the same. *Tempo is negotiable and individual to each player.*

Many golfers try to make a concerted effort to slow down their backswings, but in my experience many golfers' backswings are already too slow. That's right, too slow, and it can disturb the rhythm of the swing. I stumbled upon this idea of a slow backswing and abrupt downswing by accident in my own swing. I was reviewing videotapes of my practice swings versus my swings when I was hitting a ball. The practice swings I was taking were made to try to match the clubhead speed I would normally generate with the club when hitting the ball. The difference in the practice swings and actual swings at the ball was that the amount of time it took for the club to get to the top of my backswing was much faster and my backswing was longer in the practice swing. But because my backswing was very slow and much shorter when I was hitting the ball, I tended to try to ineffectively force the acceleration of the club on the downswing. My swing was slow in the beginning and then made a very abrupt change in pace at the transition into the downswing. Once I discovered this, I worked on feeling that my backswing and downswing are a similar pace and the entire swing is one continuous motion, an idea that I believe can help many golfers. When I do this, as a result of improving the overall pace of my swing, my rhythm and timing also improve. It doesn't make any sense to go back slowly and then come

Thinking about making the backswing very slow can lead to a very fast, abrupt change in direction, disturbing the smoothness and tempo of the swing.

down quickly on the downswing. This movement can produce the opposite sensation that most golfers should be striving for, a swing that feels fluid and blends the body and the arms together.

One example of the benefits of good rhythm is that it can help

When pulling the wagon, as long as the pulling motion of the movement is constant, the rope remains taut and there is no slack. If there is any sudden movement, such as an abrupt slowdown in walking pace, the rope slackens and the wagon catches up to the person pulling it. If the person stops walking, the wagon passes him or her.

improve the blending and relationship of your arms and body. This is especially true in the downswing, when the angles must be maintained in order to store power. These angles can be disturbed by any sudden quick movement or slowing down of the body, causing the arms to lose the relationship with the body. Imagine a person walking and pulling a little wagon with a rope. As long as the pulling motion of the movement is constant, the rope remains taut and there is no slack. If there is any sudden move-

ment, such as an abrupt slowdown in walking pace, the rope slackens and the wagon catches up to the person. If the person stops walking, just as if the body stops rotating on the downswing, the wagon passes him or her at the point where the arms would pass the body, causing the connection between the body and arms to be lost. Or if the person pulling the wagon suddenly jerks his or her arm forward, the rope and wagon will pass him or her. Similarly, if the golfer suddenly accelerates his or her arms faster than his or her body is rotating, the relationship between the arms and body, and hence the golf club, will be

Connection at impact. Left arm is against the chest, with the body supporting the swinging of the left arm.

lost. A sound thought may be to sense a smooth and uninterrupted downswing without any sudden starts or stops.

Earlier I talked about the danger of trying to keep the right arm close to the body in an effort to connect it to the body. But connection with the left arm can also be very helpful in learning to work the arms and body together, as well as maintaining and releasing the angles. I was first exposed to this idea when I read Jimmy Ballard's book, *How to Perfect your Golf Swing*, and later when I visited the Jimmy Ballard Academy. The story behind the "connection theory" is that Sam Byrd, the first professional baseball player to win a PGA Tour event, learned it from the legendary Babe Ruth. Byrd and Ruth were roommates for many years. Ruth enjoyed playing golf and always maintained that the baseball swing and golf swing were virtually the same, just on a different plane. Ruth always practiced his batting with a handkerchief, keeping it between his chest and the inside part of his arm. Byrd tried this with his golf swing and had some success; thus, the theory was born. Sam Byrd later shared

this concept with Jimmy Ballard.

One of the main thrusts of Ballard's theory is that the left arm should

To correctly perform the connection exercise with an object, the left arm must be in front and on top of the chest. Avoid putting the object under your armpit in a way that causes the left arm to be attached to your side.

A shirtsleeve can be used to help maintain the arm/body relationship, even while playing, by pulling out the armpit part of the shirt and putting it between the chest and the left arm.

Vijay Singh, on the range practicing connection with a small towel.

stay connected to the chest throughout the swing, until the arm is pulled off the chest at the finish position. In essence, the body is supporting the swinging of the left arm. You can experience this by holding a small towel or headcover between the underside of the left arm and the chest, keeping it there throughout the swing, and then letting it fall out at the finish position. To perform this exercise correctly, the left arm must be in front of your chest. Avoid putting the object under your armpit in a way that causes the left arm to be attached to your side. I've also seen professionals use their shirtsleeve to help maintain this relationship, pulling out the armpit part of the shirt and putting it between the chest and the left arm while playing. Start out by taking some swings, baseball style, swinging the club back and through with the club horizontal to the ground and about chest-high, feeling the connection of the left arm to the chest throughout the motion. You can also experiment with the swinging and hitting methods as you do this exercise. Doing this will further your understanding of the relationship between the arms and the body.

After doing the exercise baseball style, take your normal setup and start to take some three-quarter length swings, eventually becoming comfortable enough to hit some short shots. Maintaining the relationship between the left arm and the chest prevents "slack" or "dis-

If the arms lose their connection to the body, they will separate from it; the object will fall out early and may produce a "chicken wing" effect.

connection" and should give you a sense of how the body and arms can work together in the golf swing. If the arms separate from the body too early, the object falls out and the lag is lost. This, in essence, is what the "chicken wing" effect is. When the left arm is excessively bent after impact, it is because the arms lose their connected relationship with the body, and, in essence, pass the body. But as long as the left arm stays connected to the chest, the relationship between the left arm and chest remains intact, and the object will remain in place during the follow-through position and then fall out as the left arm nears the finish position and naturally comes off the chest.

Another effective exercise to work on your rhythm and blending your arm and body motion is to take full swings at a slow pace. Let's say you normally hit a seven iron 140 yards. Taking a full swing, try to hit the ball 90 yards. Make sure you are taking a full swing. This will require you to make what feels like a "slow motion" swing. Once you can hit it 90 yards, making solid contact, try to hit it 100 yards. Then, keep increasing in increments. This exercise does several things. Remember how we learn to do physical skills slowly before doing them at higher speeds? This practice helps you master your full swing motion at slower speeds. Swinging at fast speeds and then trying to slow down and smooth out the motion is less effective than starting slowly and smoothly and then building up speed. This exercise lets you experience how much energy is needed to hit the ball the desired distance. We've all experienced the swing, when laying up short of the water or other hazard, where we made a nice smooth effortless swing and witnessed the ball go much farther than we anticipated, sometimes too far and in the water. In addition, this exercise helps smooth

When the arms stay connected to the body, the object remains intact through impact.

out the very crucial transition phase from the backswing into the downswing. It should be your goal to perform this exercise and be able to hit shots with a full swing, at any speed, solid and with good direction control. I agree with Homer Kelly when he said in his book, *The Golfing Machine*, "An inability to execute a full pivot stroke (full swing) at one half and one quarter speed as smoothly as at full speed indicates a flaw in the full speed procedure."

I believe that to a certain degree learning new things or breaking old habits is the challenge of timing and sequencing the movements and then incorporating them into our natural tempo. Many times this is what creates the difficulty and challenge of incorporating new swing changes. Sometimes I give a player something to work on that doesn't necessarily show immediate improvement, but I know that after the player learns to coordinate and time the sequence, improvement will take place. For example, sometimes a player can benefit by shortening his or her backswing. It's not that the movement of shortening the swing is difficult, but rather learning to sequence and time the motion from a different position at the top and getting comfortable with it is what takes time. Making changes is as much about incorporating those changes from the sequencing and timing perspective as it is about getting comfortable with something new.

However, sometimes the real killers of tempo and rhythm are not physical, but rather take place in our minds and usually manifest themselves in the form of anxiety and fear. This can have a detrimental, and at times devastating, effect on our ability to perform. This is why the mental game needs to be addressed, because no matter how good our swings are, anxious and negative feelings and thoughts happen to all golfers and can have a severely adverse effect on our tempo, rhythm, and timing. Although I understand a great deal about the mental side of the game, it is not my area of expertise. There is, however, helpful material available on this aspect of the game. I highly recommend Dr. Bob Rotella's book, *Golf is Not a Game of Perfect*. It's a short and easy read that addresses all of the mental aspects of the game, including anxiety's effect on performance.

In the end, improving your ability to swing the club with good rhythm and tempo is most likely a combination of improving both your swing mechanics and your mental approach to the game.

Playing the Short Shots

J ust as we learn to take little steps before taking bigger ones, it is also very helpful for golfers to learn to use a golf club effectively and understand its relationship with the ball with short shots. Many golfers talk about the importance of the short game for scoring because more than 60% of the game is played inside 100 yards. We've all experienced days where we hit the ball poorly but our short game saved us and still allowed us to produce a fairly good score. Although this chapter covers the short game, including chip shots, pitch shots, lob shots, and bunker play, its main focus is on the small swings. These will help improve how you use the club, which in turn will help improve your full swing since much of what you learn with the smaller swings will become building blocks that can be transferred and incorporated into the full swing.

CHIP SHOTS

As with all approach shots to the green, the goal of chipping is to get the ball as close to the hole (if not in the hole) as possible. And it's a great feeling when you hit a chip shot so close to the pin that your friends say, "That's good, you don't need to putt that." But how do you develop the "feel" and "touch" around the greens to increase the frequency of shots hit very close to the hole? Many think that frequent practice leads to good touch. Practice certainly helps, but it's of no help if your contact—how solid you hit your short shots—is inconsistent, something most golfers struggle with to a certain degree. The force with which the club is swung needs to be consistently transferred from the club to the ball to develop consistent distance control. Anyone who struggles with distance control is suffering primarily with contact issues. It's impossible to develop distance control if a golfer's clubhead hits behind the ball on one shot, hits the top of the ball on the next, hits the middle of the ball on the next, then finally strikes the ball solidly on the next one. Even with the same amount of force, none of these shots will go the same direction and distance. If you hit a solid five iron, say 165 yards, how far will it go if you miss the sweet spot? Not 165 yards. And the short game is much more precise than that. If the goal of the short game is to get the ball close to the hole every time, your technique must produce consistent contact to obtain consistent results. Tour players have great touch around the greens, an ability to hit any short shot, from any lie or condition, close to the hole from varying distances. They have all developed the ability to make consistent, solid contact with the ball a very high percentage of the time.

How good is your contact? Here's a simple test that doesn't require you to even hit a ball. Take a look at these two lies.

TIGHT LIE   FLUFFY LIE

One of them is considered a "tight lie" on a very short, mowed fairway. The other one is a lie on the first cut of very light rough. Which lie do you prefer? And what don't you like about the other lie? Most golfers answer that they like the lie in the light rough, whether chipping or hitting a full shot. The reason most golfers like this lie is that their contact is not as good as it needs to be.

Golfers are told to "hit down on the ball." Technically, this suggestion is about angle of attack, or how sharply downward the club is heading into the ball relative to the ground. By itself, does this idea help your understanding? Probably not. The short game, as with all shots, has another relationship that needs to be understood—the relationship between the club and the ground. In the photo below, the clubhead is approaching impact. Assuming a divot will be taken, where should the club actually start to make contact with the ground?

I am astounded that the answer many golfers give to this question is that the divot starts one or two inches behind the ball or just before

or under the ball. The correct answer is after the ball is hit; the club first strikes the ball and then the club contacts the ground. If you think the divot starts before the ball, look at it this way: If you hit the ground first, the ground absorbs the energy of the clubhead and then the ground transfers energy to the ball. That transfer of energy some-times results in the ball moving only a couple of yards on a full shot, what is described as a "fat" or "heavy" shot. In essence, the bottom of the arc that the clubhead travels is the bottom of the divot. In fact, this happens with every shot, except with a driver off of a tee, although the longer the club is, the shallower and smaller the divot. Another important thing about divots: they're a great form of feed-back because they tell you a lot about your clubhead path relative to your target. For example, if you see the divot pointing straight to the left, the club is swinging from outside in. Players who swing from outside in tend to have a relatively steep angle of approach, which creates divots that tend to be deeper and larger and point to the left. Players who swing too much from the inside tend to have a shallower angle of approach and take shallower divots that point to the right.

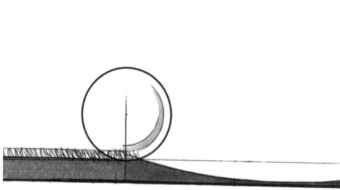

The bottom of the divot is the low point of the clubhead's downward arc.

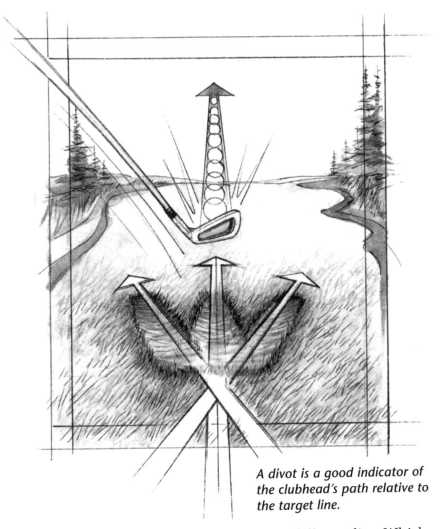

A divot is a good indicator of the clubhead's path relative to the target line.

Let's go back to the picture with the two different lies. Which one did you like? I'm sure many of you picked the fluffy lie as opposed to the tight lie. Your preference says a lot. The fluffy lie, the one in the light rough, provides a cushion and allows for a much greater degree of error than does the lie from the very closely mown area. The tight lie allows for very little, if any, margin for error. Most golfers also prefer that same fluffy lie for full shots. However, highly skilled players will choose the tight lie because it allows them the ability to make clean contact with the golf ball, giving them more control over its spin and flight. Higher-handicap players like the fluffy lie because the cushion under the ball allows a greater margin for error, thereby making it an easier shot. If you don't like the tight lie, chances are that the club/ball contact with your shots in your short game, as well as your long game, needs improvement. In fact, it most likely reveals that many times your club hits the ground before the ball, with the club-head skipping off the ground and into the ball, or digging in and causing the fat shot. Or your fear, conscious or subconscious, that you'll hit the ground first causes you to inevitably hit the middle or the top of the ball, neither of which produces acceptable results. In addition, many golfers do much better on artificial turf, such as the mats at the driving range, than on natural grass. The primary reason is that these golfers hit the ground before the ball and when this happens on artificial turf, the clubhead skips off the turf and into the ball, producing a reasonable shot. However, on grass this same contact would have the clubhead digging into the ground, producing a much less desirable result.

Let's learn to improve the way you use the golf club by making some observations and using feedback with a basic chip shot. We'll start with a pitching wedge from a tightly mown area. One of the most critical elements of chipping is ball position. Some latitude exists with regard to ball position, but to start, place the ball just inside your right instep. Set up with your feet somewhat close together and with a little more weight on your left side than your right. While this setup is not mandatory, it will encourage a sharper, steeper angle of approach, which promotes hitting "down on the ball" and striking the ground after the ball. It's fine if you prefer to set up and align slightly open with your stance and hips. However, for those of you, like myself, who prefer to have your feet pointing more

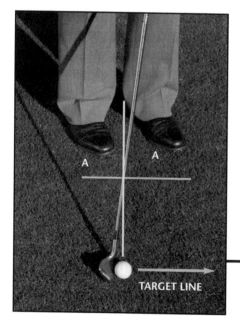

TARGET LINE

Pointing the feet toward the target (A) can create a false illusion of where the ball is positioned in the stance.

toward the target, I must warn that this type of stance, although perfectly acceptable, creates an illusion with regard to ball position. The ball can appear to be back in the stance when it is actually forward of center in the stance.

If you really struggle with the tight lie, go ahead and hit shots from some slightly longer grass, but not from heavy rough. You can graduate to the more difficult lie later. The first goal, when hitting these chip shots, is to focus on swinging the club downward, making contact first with the ball and then the ground. Because these are short chip shots, and the club is not moving with a lot of force, you won't be taking any big divots as visual feedback and thus have to make a concerted effort to hear the club hitting, or "brushing," the ground after the ball is struck. A ball being struck first, as opposed to the ground being struck first, has a very distinctly different sound. Once you can distinguish the difference, this auditory feedback can be very helpful.

The second goal when hitting this short shot is to have the shaft leaning forward through impact, or what I refer to as shaft-lean. In the Elements of Speed chapter, I briefly mentioned how at impact the

---

The handle leans forward through impact regardless of the shot, whether the lie is level (1), uneven (2), in the rough (3), or playing out of the trees (4).

handle (grip) of a club should be slightly forward of the clubhead. This is the natural design of the golf club. The handle in front of the clubhead at impact is something that is evident in nearly every shot played by a skilled player from any situation, whether it's the middle of the fairway or a shot played from the trees. However, to start learning to use the club in this manner on a full shot can be extremely challenging and less effective than first learning to use it with a short shot. When the golf club is used as it is designed to be, shaft-lean at impact improves ball contact. It also consistently lofts the ball at the same trajectory, another important aspect of learning distance control.

When a golfer hits a short shot and the shaft is not leaning forward through impact, the outcome is usually observed in the form of the wrists breaking down. This effect can be witnessed in the short swings, as well as the long, of a very high percentage of golfers. This ineffective motion causes either a heavy or bladed shot, and even when hit relatively solid will launch the ball at inconsistent tra-

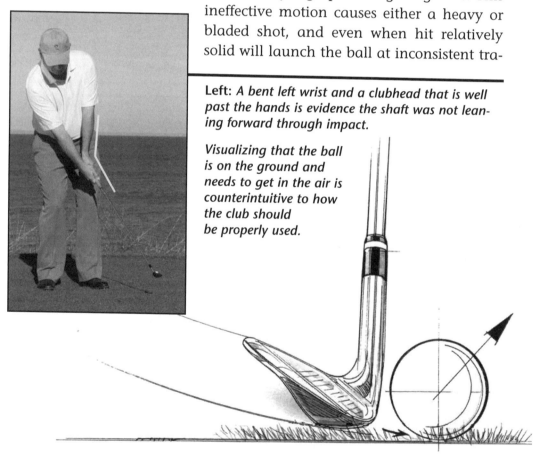

Left: *A bent left wrist and a clubhead that is well past the hands is evidence the shaft was not leaning forward through impact.*

Visualizing that the ball is on the ground and needs to get in the air is counterintuitive to how the club should be properly used.

*The chip shot exercise. The ball is positioned back in the stance (1);
the hands are forward of the clubhead in backswing (2); the shaft leans forward
through impact (3); then at the finish position the hands are past the left hip,
the left arm is in line with the shaft, and the majority of weight is on the left
foot (4).*

jectories, making distance control much more difficult. I believe the primary reason for this motion is mental, not physical. The ball is on the ground, and we need to get it in the air. That basic observation causes this type of motion because logically the golfer tries to "scoop" or slide the clubhead under the ball to get the ball to go up in the air. I believe this is another example of the game being counterintuitive. When golfers do scoop the ball and allow the clubhead to pass the grip through impact, inevitably they either think, or receive the suggestion to "Take the right hand out of the shot." The right hand often gets blamed, but many times it's an illusion and is not the cause of the breaking down of the wrists. This is where rhythm, the sequencing of the action, can make the difference between an effective and ineffective motion. One significant difference you can see between the two is the position of the handle of the club and both hands at the finish position. When the wrists break down, many times the hands and the handle are still in front of the body and are not past the left hip. The finish position with a more effective technique has all of them past

If the body (A), pulls the hands/handle (B), then the clubhead (C) will be behind the hands/handle through impact. The left wrist is flat at impact.

the body. Other differences can also be noted. With the less effective use of the club, many times at the finish position the player's weight will be more on his or her right side than on the left. This is usually caused by the player starting with too much weight on his or her right side at the setup position, and the weight remains there during the motion. Or the player is falling back onto the right side during the motion, which also contributes to this ineffective motion. At the finish, when the club is used effectively, the left wrist is flat, the right wrist is slightly bent, and the clubshaft is in line with the left forearm. In addition, both arms are straight at the follow-through position, which, of course, for this short shot is also the finish position.

Mike Hebron once shared a great analogy with me to explain how the sequencing can be disrupted and how the club can pass the hands through impact. Imagine you are driving your car and have a book on the front seat of the car. If you slam on the brakes, the book flies off the seat and goes forward. This is similar to the red wagon illustration I gave earlier. When the hands stop moving, the clubhead passes the hands. One way to keep the hands moving is with the pivot. We can look at it as an ABC sequence, with the letter A on the body, B on the hands/grip of club, and C on the clubhead. On the forward swing, the body (A) moves first and as it continues to move, it pulls the arms, which in turn pull the wrists and hands/grip (B), which in turn pull the clubhead (C) through impact and to the finish position. This is a swinging motion, with the pivoting action of the body doing most of the work and acting as the main power source, pulling the arms, hands, and club through impact. Sensing the connection between the left arm and the body can also be helpful. Notice there is a small pivot and a small arm swing; it's just a smaller version of the full swing.

When working on preventing the wrists from breaking down through impact, often golfers focus on keeping the left wrist flat, but sometimes I find it more helpful for them to focus on keeping their right wrist bent. Another suggestion is to solely focus on the movement of the golf club; have the grip or shaft leaning forward toward the target as it is moving through impact, as opposed to thinking about the clubhead, which for most is not a good focal point. Think of it as a race to the ball, with the grip end beating the clubhead. Years ago, Eddie Merrins in the book, *Swing the Handle, Not the Clubhead* presented this positive way of approaching the movement of the club by thinking about moving the handle, or the grip of the club, as opposed to the clubhead.

Many times golfers learning to keep the shaft leaning forward through impact will use an unnecessary amount of muscular tension to get the desired results. Here is a really effective exercise to learn shaft-lean and monitor muscle tension; using a five iron, grip down on the iron so that your hands are low on the club, with your right hand touching part of the shaft, if necessary. When you set up, play the ball back in the stance and lean the shaft forward, so that the grip is up against the inside of your left forearm. You may need to stand a little closer to the ball with the longer club so that the shaft is more vertical and the heel is a little off the ground. Now, hit a chip shot and try to keep the grip on your left forearm throughout the motion. Don't worry about the flight of the ball; it will barely get off the ground because of the lack of loft on the club. At the finish, make sure the grip is still touching your forearm. As a result of this, you'll experience the left wrist flat and the right wrist still bent, both arms straight, and the left forearm in line with the clubshaft; an effective follow-through position. The real challenge in doing this exercise is to be able to do it without any tension in the arms, wrists, or hands. Monitor your

Shaft-lean and muscle tension exercise. Using a five iron, and with the ball back in the stance, grip down on the iron near the shaft and hold the grip of the club against the left forearm (left), and keep it there throughout the motion and at the finish position (right). Note flat left wrist (insets).

tension at the finish position with this exercise and anytime you are practicing your chipping technique. Keep working on it until you can do it with a minimal amount of tension. This exercise can be done with excessive tension and still produce positive results because the club is functioning the way it is designed. As a result, contact and trajectory are much more consistent, thereby improving accuracy with both direction and distance. The problem with using excessive muscular tension is that it becomes difficult to effectively use this technique as you start to make bigger swings and move toward your full swing. As you work on your short swing technique it's good to have a target, but at first don't become overly focused on trying to get the ball close to a specific target.

The focus when working on these small swings with a pitching wedge should be to swing the club on a downward angle of approach, which ensures that the club/ball/ground contact has the shaft leaning forward through impact with both arms straight, the left forearm in line with the clubshaft, and the majority of weight on the left side at the follow-through/finish position. Once you can successfully perform these short chips with your pitching wedge, try other clubs with the same exact motion, experimenting with all of your clubs from a six iron through your sand wedge. You can even try this motion with a hybrid club. Try different lies. Mixing it up and playing different clubs from different lies will help create a repertoire of shots from which to choose when you are playing and facing different situations.

PITCH SHOTS

Once you are successful with the short chip, it's time to move to a little bigger swing, such as one you would use for a short pitch shot. For this shot, use something more lofted like a gap or sand wedge. You can adjust your setup for a pitch shot with your feet a little farther apart, but not as far apart as for a full short-iron shot. The ball position for a standard pitch shot can be just forward of the center of your stance and should not, at any time, be played forward of this position, as the bottom of the arc is not forward of this point. If the ball is played more forward than this, the club will hit the ground before the ball unless the player makes some unnecessary compensations. However, this shot can be played from ball positions farther back in the stance. For a really low shot, I play the ball back off the inside of my right foot. The farther back in the stance the ball is played, the more the shaft needs to lean forward, the less effective loft the club will have, and the lower the ball trajectory will be. For this exercise, position the ball slightly back of center in the stance and slightly lean the grip and shaft forward toward the target. Take the club back only to the point where the shaft is parallel to the ground. Hit this shot with the same two goals: (1) contact with the ground after the ball, with the shaft leaning forward through and past impact, and (2) finish with the left wrist flat and the right wrist still slightly bent, with the majority of weight on the left side. Because it is a bigger swing with more force, try to make some small divots. When you hold the finish position, try to feel a minimal amount of tension in your arms and wrists. Take note that the length of the follow-through/finish position is a little abbreviated compared to the length of the backswing. However, swinging the clubhead downward and into the ground will make the abbreviated finish easier and more natural. If your finish is too long, reduce the length of your backswing or the speed at which

The pitch shot exercise. The ball is positioned slightly back of center, with the shaft leaning forward (1). On the backswing, the club moves back to parallel to the ground (2); the shaft leans forward through impact (3); and at the follow-through/finish position the shaft is in line with the hands (4).

you are trying to swing the club. Don't try to hit the ball a specific distance; just try to make the proper motion. You're still using a swinging motion; the pivot has just become a little bigger.

The other source-of-power technique I discussed earlier is hitting. Remember, hitting is accomplished in unison with the rotation of the body, but uses the right arm to provide more power than in the swinging motion. The movement of the right arm is sometimes referred to as right arm thrust, a phrase that I first saw in Homer Kelly's book.

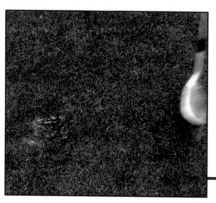

This short pitch shot is a good shot with which to start experiencing the hitting technique. For this shot, in the backswing the player creates the angle of the right arm. You'll notice the body has not pivoted very much, the club is back mostly through the bending of the right arm. Then, on the forward swing, the

Small swings create small divots.

right arm is straightened downward through impact. There is some body rotation, but the main source of power is the right arm. The right arm is using a sort of piston motion, with the player purposely bending and then straightening the right arm. With this movement, the right hand needs to feel as if it is going down toward the ground, not forward toward the target. The finish position will look very similar to the swinging motion. Because most golfers have never experienced this technique, it may take a few shots to correctly perform it. The hitting method can be especially effective with short shots around the green.

Experiment with different ball positions and with either or both power source techniques, moving the ball a little forward and a little back in the setup, and see how the ball responds in trajectory, spin, and roll. Experiment with these ideas from different types of lies. Try some different clubs. For example, take a three or four iron and place the ball way back in your stance, just inside the right heel. This is the shot to play when you need a really low trajectory recovery shot to get out of the woods. By doing this, you're using your imagination and

The hitting motion for a pitch shot. The ball is positioned back in the stance at setup (1); the right arm bends in the backswing (2) and straightens through impact (3); both arms are straight at the follow-through/finish position, with the shaft in line with the left forearm (4).

creating different shots with the same club, building a toolbox for different shots at different times.

THE BRIDGE SWING

Next, we're going to work on making a bigger swing, what I refer to as a "bridge" swing. I call it that because it can act as the learning bridge between a pitch shot and the full swing. Set up with a stance width close to or the same as you would for a full short iron shot, with the ball positioned just forward of center in the stance. Next, make a swing where your left arm is basically parallel to the ground in the backswing, with the left forearm and clubshaft creating an "L." On the forward swing finish with the right arm parallel to the ground, creating another "L", and nearly all of the weight on the left side. In this swing, the body pivot is a little bigger and the angles with the arms and wrists are also greater. These angles are expanded through impact and then re-created at the finish position. Many golfers focus on the position in the full swing, where the angles are being re-created and the forearms appear to be "rolling" or "crossing over", a position similar to the finish position of the bridge swing. But the reality is that everything past the point of the follow-through, if performed

The Bridge swing. The left arm and clubshaft create an "L" on the backswing, then the right arm and clubshaft create another "L" at the finish position.

Right: *The forearms "roll over" and angles are re-created after the follow-through position.*

Far Right and Below: *Golfers have swings unique to themselves; therefore the exact point at which the angles of the wrists and arms are recreated on the forward swing can vary. The intended ball flight will also influence how quickly the clubface rotates after impact.*

correctly, is just a result of all that preceded it, an effective rotation of the body coupled with an effective release of the angles. After the follow-through, the right arm swings across the chest, the left arm naturally folds, and the wrists begin to re-hinge. However, because golfers have different motions, such as how they use their arms and rotate their body, the exact points at which these angles are re-created are different with every player. Therefore, the second "L" at the finish position is just a guideline; it doesn't have to be exact at this point, but rather the idea is to help you have the shaft lean forward through impact and experience re-creating angles later in your forward swing.

If you prefer, when you start doing these swings, you can hit from a little fluffier lie or tee it up very low to the ground. The idea is to focus on making the motion. Continue focusing on having the handle lead the clubhead through impact, hitting down on the ball, and taking a small divot. This is a great length swing to work on blending the rotation of your body with the swinging of your arms. You can also work on swinging the club the same distance back and through, but vary the speed with which you swing the club, hitting the shot varying distances.

Once you have learned the fundamentals and effective movement of the golf club with short chip and pitch shots, you can apply those skills to other shots that you face in the short game. Next, work with a more challenging, but fun shot: the high floating "flop," or lob shot.

LOB SHOTS

The lob shot is used when you are close to a green that has a bunker, water, or heavy rough between you and it and the hole is close to the edge of the green. The situation demands that you hit the shot high, a short distance, with a minimal amount of roll once it hits the ground. To perform this shot, most golfers would suggest positioning the ball way forward in the stance, taking a stance open to the target, and then taking a big, long, fluid swing. This is an accepted style for playing this shot; however, if you don't practice it a lot, it's more difficult to master

When opening the clubface to create more loft, first open the clubface, and then take your grip.

Right: *For the lob shot, the ball should be placed just forward of center in the stance.*

Far Right: *Playing the ball well forward in the stance moves the bottom of the arc of the swing unnaturally forward, causing the need for unnecessary and problematic compensations.*

When the clubface is open and the body is aligned parallel to the target line, (1) the clubface points to the right. Aligning the body open, left of parallel to the target line, (2) offsets the open clubface.

and unnecessary. I'm going to show you another, possibly less risky and easier way to play this shot, and then you can decide how you would like to play it.

Loft creates more height; and the more speed applied by the club to the ball, the higher the ball goes. Take your most lofted wedge, open your clubface, and then take your grip. Don't take your grip and then turn your hands to open the clubface, as this is the same as not opening the clubface. Position the ball just forward of center in your stance. The higher you want to hit this shot, the farther forward the ball position should be. But keep in mind that a ball position that is too far forward in the stance causes the problems I mentioned earlier, because the ball is now positioned forward of the bottom of the arc, where the divot should be. When you set up with your alignment parallel to the target line, you will notice that the face angle is now pointing to the right. We already know that face angle is the dominant factor in determining the direction in which the ball will fly. Thus, if you hit this shot with no other adjustments, the

ball will go to the right. This is the reason why you need to turn and align your body and stance to the left. This realignment is needed to offset the direction of the open clubface. The amount the face points to the right is the amount you need to offset by turning your body to the left. For example, if the ball lands four yards right of the flag, you

Start out mastering the lob shot with small swings, making sure the shaft leans forward through impact, with the end of the swing being the follow-through position.

Even when a very high ball trajectory is required, the clubshaft leans forward through impact.

then need to adjust by aligning yourself four yards to the left. Of course, with this open-stance setup, the clubface still needs to point a little to the right of the flag because the clubhead path will pull the ball a little to the left. With this setup, go ahead and hit some shots, making the same little swings that you were making with the short pitch shot, focusing on maintaining the shaft leaning forward through impact and a follow-through/finish position that has both arms straight and the shaft in line with the left forearm. Not maintaining shaft-lean is one of the reasons golfers struggle with this shot; they try to slide the clubhead under the ball to make it fly higher in the air, encouraging the clubhead to pass the handle at and through impact. The small pitch shot swing will produce short, high shots. If you need the ball to go higher and farther, just swing the club faster, or make a little bigger swing, utilizing the bridge swing that you just learned. With this exercise, along with understanding face angle and loft, you can learn how speed can be applied with different styles. You can make the ball go the same height and distance with a smaller, faster motion, as you can with a bigger, slower swing. Start experimenting with this shot from the fluffy or light rough first, and then challenge yourself to the tight fairway lie. You need very good technique to hit this shot off of a tight lie, but it can be done.

SAND GAME

The sand game is both different and the same as any other shot. I've combined all of the most common tips for playing a greenside bunker shot into one:

Dig in your feet, weaken your grip, open the clubface, open your stance, set the wrists early, use a steeper "V" swing for higher shots, a "U"-shaped swing for lower shots, swing your club from out to in, hit the sand so that the sand will move the ball, and let the distance of your finish control the length of the shot.

Did I miss anything? It's said that the greenside bunker shot is one of the easiest in golf. With all these tips, it certainly doesn't seem like it would be. And if it is so easy, why does the average golfer still find it so difficult; and why is it the weakest, most feared part of many golfers' games? I think the reason is that no other single part of the game has been made more complicated than the bunker game.

The primary difference between playing out of the sand versus playing on the grass is the ball/club/ground relationship. For the bunker shot, instead of trying to make the divot after the ball, you need to make the club contact the sand before the ball. In a sense, you make the divot before the ball as opposed to after the ball. In the last sections, you learned how to chip and, by making bigger swings, how to pitch the ball. Now, you

Sand wedges are designed with bounce to prevent the clubhead from digging into the sand.

are going to take that same technique and apply it to your sand game. I must emphasize that you need to have a wedge that is designed with bounce to play out of the sand. Most wedges designed for the sand are between 56 and 58 degrees and are designed with bounce; the angle between the leading edge and back edge of the sole prevents the clubface from digging deeply into the sand. Talk to your golf professional if you have questions about bounce, the best wedge for your game, and the type of sand at your course, as well as other ways you use your wedge for shots outside of the bunker. These factors can affect your decision when purchasing a wedge.

In my experience, nearly all of the golfers I work with have the same primary problem: where and how consistently their club makes contact with the sand. In fact, I can't recall giving a bunker lesson where this was not one of the issues. We've already established that making consistent contact is paramount so that the proper amount of clubhead speed can be applied for the distance for the shot at hand. With bunker shots, you need to hit the same spot in the sand every

To check where your club is entering the sand, draw a line in the sand about two inches behind the ball (left), then hit a shot. Most golfers hit too far behind the line, taking too much sand (right).

time. If you take more sand, hitting four or five inches before the ball, you'll need more speed to create more force to move that amount of sand and the ball than if you strike the sand only two inches behind the ball. More sand requires more force. *The most important thing is to strike the same spot and the same amount of sand consistently.*

Let's put you to the test to see where you strike the sand. If you don't have anywhere to practice your sand play, you may need to do this when playing nine holes later in the evening when no one else is on the course. You can do this while you are actually playing, but keep in mind that touching the sand is against the rules. You decide. Set up in the bunker like you normally would and with the grip end of your club, draw a line in the sand about two inches behind the ball, which is about one ball's width plus the width of the line the end of the grip will make when you draw the line in the sand. Make sure the line is at least a foot long. Hit a shot. Where did the club strike the sand? If you are like nearly all of the golfers I work with, your club struck the sand somewhere between four and 10 inches behind the ball. Hitting this far before the ball is ineffective, requires a lot of force, and is the primary reason golfers fail to extricate the ball from the bunker. Some of you are reading this and saying to yourselves that this is not your problem. You believe you take too little sand and the club ends up making direct contact with the ball, sending the ball on a line drive over the green. But there is a good chance your feedback is inaccurate and confusing you. Nearly all the golfers who come to me with this analysis are wrong. What is actually happening is that the club hits the sand so far behind the ball that the club actually bounces up off the sand, causing the club to make direct contact with the equator of the ball. But the golfer, not feeling the sand, only feels and hears the club contact the ball. Conservatively speaking, more than 90% of golfers I've worked with take too much sand, hitting too far behind the ball.

Since taking too much sand is the primary issue for most golfers, focus on it with this exercise. Draw two several-feet long lines in the sand about two inches apart. The line closer to your target represents the ball and the other line represents where you want the club to contact the sand. On one end, you can set up a few balls on the ball line. I've chosen the distance of two inches, but that's not carved in stone;

it's a suggestion and depends on the texture of the bunkers you are playing. But I do believe between two and three inches is best for most bunker shots. It's also important to understand that the closer to the ball you contact the sand, the more the clubface is in contact with the ball, resulting in more backspin. This is also the reason why the bunker shot is a little more forgiving than other shots. I remember the tour player Nick Price saying that the bunker shot is easier because if you err closer to the ball, the ball carries farther in the air, but has more spin and stops more quickly. Conversely, if you err and hit a little farther behind the ball, the ball may not carry as far, but it won't have as much spin and will roll farther once it hits the ground. Hence, this is why it can be said that it is the easiest and most forgiving shot in golf.

When you set up in the bunker, first dig your feet in the sand a little bit to get better footing. Don't overdo it. Set up so that the ball line is just inside your left heel and your point of contact line for the sand is just forward of the middle of your stance. In the sand, you need to make the divot before the ball, and thus need to move the ball more forward in the stance to just about inside the left heel, making our point of entry about two inches behind the ball. Take your normal grip, but don't open the clubface; for now just leave the clubface square. Start on the one end, without the balls, and focus on taking shallow divots with the club contacting and removing the first line in the sand. It's important that you try to make the divots shallow, not deep. Start with small swings at first, similar in length to the swings when hitting a short pitch shot. Be sure to maintain the shaft-lean through impact and into the follow-through, just as you do with other shots. Not maintaining forward shaft-lean is one of the main reason golfers hit too far behind the ball. I also believe this is caused by the idea of needing to hit the sand to lift the ball out of the bunker. Once

Start out mastering the sand game hitting short shots by taking small swings with a square clubface (left), making sure the shaft leans forward through impact, with the end of the swing being the follow-through position (right).

you can consistently contact the line, move toward the spot where the balls and the contact line behind them are. Keep the clubface square and hit some shots. Don't try to hit the ball a specific distance; just make the small pitch shot backswing and follow-through. The ball will fly relatively low because the face is square, so make sure you do this exercise where the face of the bunker is not very steep. When you do this correctly, using the point of contact as your feedback, you will be amazed at how easy it is, and how little effort it takes, to hit a bunker shot.

After some success with these exercises, you'll learn the trajectory that the ball flies with the face being square. We have already learned how to hit a high lob shot off of the grass. A bunker shot that requires a higher trajectory is no different. Open the clubface more to add loft and create a higher trajectory, and then adjust your stance and body alignment by opening it to the left to offset the amount the clubface is pointing to the right. Do the same thing you did with the lob shot. Although there is a direct correlation between the length of the swing and the length of the shot, some golfers, comparatively speaking, are

For a bunker shot, even when a very high trajectory is required, the club-shaft still leans forward through impact.

more successful with shorter, faster swings, while for others it's a longer, slower one. This is just a style preference. Continue to experiment. Open the clubface more or less. Take bigger or smaller backswings, and slower and faster down-swings. Find your own style and what works best for you.

I struggled with my bunker game for many years. It's a bad sign when you see your approach shot in the air, know its going to miss the green, and hope that it doesn't go in the bunker. And of course it does. Then, I'm standing in the bunker, hoping I don't leave the next one in the bunker or blade it over the green. During this period, I also took too much sand, sometimes as much as seven inches. I tried all of the tips that I mentioned and probably a few more. But once I under-stood that the shot is really no different than a pitch shot and that I needed to be consistent with the amount of sand I took, I turned my bunker game around. I may not be happy that my approach shot misses the green and goes into the bunker, but I have confidence and am excited at the opportunity to hit another great bunker shot.

I can't stress the importance of learning to use the club effectively with your short shots. If a golfer can't use the club effectively with a short chip, how effective will his or her use of the club be when he or she takes a full swing with a driver? We learn things little before big, and the golf swing should be no different. The true beauty of learning good technique with your short shots is not only that you'll lower your scores, but also that you'll be establishing a sound foundation for your full swing.

CHAPTER 10

Putting: The Other Game

It is sometimes said that putting is a separate and different game, and I do believe there is a lot of truth in this statement. The level of some golfers' skills on the putting green is similar to that of their ball-striking. However, I know 20-handicap golfers who would have a single-digit handicap if they hit the ball as well as they putted. The opposite is also true. I've seen five-handicappers putt, and if they hit the ball as poorly as they putted, they would be closer to a 20 handicap. Being a good ball-striker doesn't necessarily mean you'll be a good putter. Plenty of great ball-strikers in the world will never play professionally because their putting is not nearly as good as their ball-striking.

If there was one book that changed the way I approached my putting, it was *Dave Pelz's Putting Bible.* It wasn't so much the content that made the first impression, but rather a photo of a golfer. Pelz used to conduct his own world putting championships. Golfers would compete and qualify locally, then regionally, for the big final tournament to earn the title of the best putter. What's interesting is that in the finals, the golfers who competed for the titles were a very diversified group—men, women, 12-year-olds, some top amateurs, and tour players—illustrating that you can be a great putter no matter what your age or gender. Pelz's book contains pictures of the contestants, including one that left an indelible impression on me. It was a picture of one of the contestants in the finals: a 27-year-old man named Bill Rockwell. At the age of 19, Rockwell had a tragic motorcycle accident. As a result of that accident one of his arms was amputated and the other was left with no function, so Rockwell learned to putt with his foot. I couldn't believe it. He putted crouched down, gripping the put-

Despite his physical challenges, Bill Rockwell created his own unique style to be an effective putter.

ter between the toes of one foot, anchoring the grip against his hip and balancing himself with his other foot, and competed against top amateurs and tour players. So much for form, this man was all about function. This was clear evidence that a player's putting form has to be negotiable.

Fortunately, I'm a very good putter. And because putting is one of my strengths, I give a fair amount of putting lessons. Golfers think I have the secret. If a golfer comes to me for lessons and tells me that he or she is working a lot on form (stance, grip, shoulder movement, and so on), I'll start my lesson by hitting a 20-foot putt using one hand, legs crossed, and hit the ball with the toe of the putter. Although I can hit pretty good putts from this setup, I don't do it to impress the golfer. Rather, I do it to get the golfer's attention and illustrate that form is not that important, using it as a foundation to explain the laws that apply to putting.

Putting requires precision and in ways has less margin for error than do other parts of the game. Although I consider putting a differ-

ent game from the short or long game, it is not exempt from the laws of physics. The three laws involved in putting are path, face angle, and center-face hits. Ball flight laws do not really apply, because the ball is not leaving the ground. You really can't slice or hook a putt; however, you can roll the ball in a way that is less than optimal.

The trend used to be for golfers to work on the path of their clubhead throughout

Sometimes I start my lessons by hitting putts from an unusual stance to illustrate how negotiable putting form can be.

the stroke, trying to keep the head going straight back on the backswing and straight through to the finish, all the while keeping the clubface pointing at the target. This may work well for really short putts, but the fact is that as the putt gets longer and requires a longer swing, the movement of the putter head has a natural arc, one that exists with the path of every other club, inside to square to inside. Now the trend is to move the clubhead on an arc, which makes more sense to me. However, golfers need to realize that this is not something they have to force to happen, but rather something that should happen naturally as a result of the design of the putter. But how important is the path of the clubhead when striking a putt? Dave Pelz, who has done extensive studies on the laws of putting, reports that the path of the putter head only contributes about 15% to the starting direction of the golf ball. The face angle at impact, just as with all other shots, has a much greater influence than does the path of the club. I believe that too much emphasis is placed on path, causing golfers to become very methodical and mechanical with their stroke. It's easy to observe how much more important face angle is than path. From two feet away you can have an extremely unnatural path, but as long as the face is square at impact, facing the hole, the ball goes in. That same putt with a straight back and through path but with the face angle slightly open and pointing to the right at impact, causes the ball to miss to the right. I remember when back in the mid-90s I had a putting lesson with Darrell Kestner, the well-respected instructor and Champions Tour Player, and he used these same examples to show me what is important and nonnegotiable with putting.

The other law in putting is center-face hits, or putts struck on the sweet spot of the putter head. The importance of this law cannot be overstated. In a full shot, a ball struck towards the toe of a five iron does not go the same distance it would if struck on the sweet spot. The same goes for putting. A 30-foot putt when the ball is struck toward the toe or heel of the putter does not go the same distance as a putt that is struck in the center of the face. Many times I'll see a golfer hit a putt that is considerably short of the hole. The player will comment that he or she didn't hit it hard enough, but the fact is that the reason it didn't reach the hole was that the putt wasn't struck solid. In addition, hitting the ball off center influences face angle. When a putt is

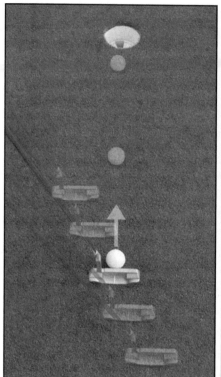 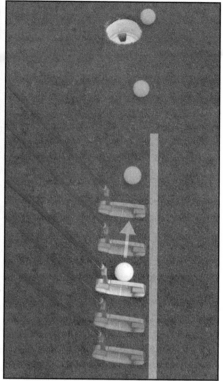

On a two-foot putt, if the putter face is pointing at the hole, even if the putter head path is extremely outside in, the ball will still go in.

On a two-foot putt, if the putter head path is straight back and straight through, but the putter face is pointing slightly right of the hole, the ball will miss to the right.

struck toward the toe, the force causes the face to open, in turn causing the starting direction of the putt to be off the intended line to the right. Toward the heel causes the face to close and the ball to start to the left of its intended line. That's why I dislike the tip about hitting the ball off the toe of the putter on fast greens and downhill putts. This could be a great idea if you hit it in the same spot on the toe every time so that you could judge how much the face opens and how much energy transfer is lost, but why would you want to do that? Instead, try to hit the ball softer.

The fact is, most golfers don't hit their putts very solidly, but many putts go in despite this fact and not because of it. Top putters hit the ball solid. To practice and learn to hit your putts more solidly, you need feedback and, especially with putting, a controlled environment. I suggest that you don't work on your putting on putting greens. Putting greens are imperfect surfaces that can cause varying results and make understanding feedback difficult, if not impossible. Even the best greens are imperfect. I remember reading that Dave Pelz tested the very smooth greens for a U.S. Open on a morning before they were walked and played on. I don't remember the exact numbers, but I believe he took a 10-foot breaking putt and, using a device he had designed that rolls the ball the same speed and direction, found that even on the proper line and speed, only 70% of the putts went in. And this was on some of the best-conditioned greens in the world. Take some solace in the fact that it's not always you that causes the putt to miss. I've integrated this idea into the mental aspect of my own putting to the point that sometimes I'll say, "I made that putt, it just didn't go in!" What I do suggest is that you practice putting on a carpet.

How fast the ball rolls on the carpet, or how it would measure on a Stimpmeter, the device used to measure the speed of greens, is not important. What is imperative is that it be a smooth and consistent surface. Shag carpet, reminiscent of the 70s, is not recommended.

Work on improving center-face hits and face angle on four-foot putts (about a driver's length). Use a quarter (or a dime for more of a challenge) on the floor to represent the hole, with a clubshaft about a foot behind it. You can also put another club down along your foot line as an alignment reference. For

A simple, yet very effective indoor putting exercise can be done on a smooth surface with two clubs, two bandages, a quarter, a putter, and a few balls.

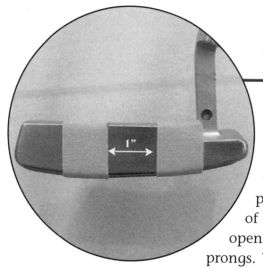

Placing two small bandages one inch apart on the putter face gives audible feedback for center-face hits.

feedback with regard to center-face hits, there are some learning devices on the market that work well. These attach to the face of the putter and have prongs on both sides of the sweet spot, allowing a small opening for the ball to hit between the prongs. When the ball is not struck on the sweet spot, the ball strikes the prong and goes practically sideways. Or you can make a homemade version. Take two small bandages and space them 1 inch apart on your putter. Try to measure the distance accurately, making the center point of the opening the sweet spot on your putter. The bandages won't give you the visual feedback that you would get from one of the learning devices you can purchase, but they'll let you feel and hear whether or not you hit the ball between them, on the sweet spot of the putter face.

As you do this exercise, don't become overly focused on path. In my own game, I don't even work on path, and unless you see your putter really moving with an abnormal clubhead path, you probably shouldn't either. The feedback for face angle is going to be your ability to roll the ball over the coin. If your face angle is open or closed at impact, the ball will miss the coin. Hitting the ball to the clubshaft behind the coin will keep some pace on the ball as it rolls over the coin. It's been proven that the highest percentage of putts that go in have enough speed that if they did miss, they would go about a foot or so past the hole. Because greens are imperfect surfaces and can be bumpy, especially around the hole where all golfers walk, putts need to have enough speed to help keep the ball on line, which in turn will lead to sinking more putts. This exercise gives you two sources of feedback in learning center-face hits. The first is your sense of touch, because when the ball hits a bandage, it feels very dead as opposed to feeling very solid when the ball is struck between them. The second is the audible feedback when the ball hits between the bandages, a nice

Right: *Hold the finish position when practicing your short putts. Left wrist flat and right wrist slightly bent indicates that the shaft was leaning slightly forward through impact.*

Left: *Even with the putter, the shaft leans slightly forward through impact. This will get the ball rolling on the ground sooner.*

clean clicking sound as opposed to the dead sound you'll hear when you hit one of the bandages.

For this exercise, a successful putt is defined as one in which the ball hits the center of the face, rolls over any part of the coin, and hits the clubshaft behind the coin. Also, if you are using a standard-length putter, hold your finish and have the shaft in line with your left arm, with the left wrist flat and the right wrist bent, just as you do with short chips. It's important that the shaft leans slightly forward through impact to decrease the loft of the putter at impact (yes, putters have 4 to 6 degrees of loft) and imparts a more efficient roll of the ball. Not doing this, especially with longer putts, can increase the loft of the putter, causing the ball to leave the ground at the beginning of the putt. This may not be visible to the player putting, but it affects the way the ball rolls since it starts out by bouncing before rolling on the ground. I also recommend, if possible, getting a second putter you can leave the device on to keep at home or in your office. (It can even be an old putter that you've retired.) You will be more inclined to do the exercise with a putter readily available. It's helpful if it's the same putter as the one you use, but that's not necessary in order for you to improve. Working short putts like these exercises builds confidence. And being confident and better at short putts is probably the best way to improve your scoring.

Look next at long putts; say more than six feet and up to 40 or so. As you perfect your contact, the amount of energy transferred from the club to the ball becomes more consistent, and over time your distance control improves dramatically. If you have space indoors, you can do the exercise from longer distances and will find it even more challenging to hit the sweet spot of the putter face. You can do some work outdoors on the practice putting green to develop a feel for the speed for the greens you play on. I strongly recommend that before you play, practice some longer putts, especially on new courses, or, if you always play different courses, to get a feel for the speed. But I don't believe spending hours on the putting green hitting longer putts improves your long putting if you're not hitting your putts solid.

A golfer can hit very solid putts, but if his or her read of the amount of break or the speed to match it is wrong, the putt won't go in. However, hitting your putts solid and on their intended line will also help your green-reading skills, as you will now be hitting your putts on a consistent line and speed. One reason golfers read greens differently is that they are subconsciously compensating for a less than perfect putting stroke. A right-handed golfer will tend to read a right-to-left breaking putt with more break than another golfer if his or her tendency is to pull putts to the left. This is one reason you should be careful when having others help you read your putts.

Of course, the importance of the mental side of putting can't be ignored or understated. How a player thinks and what his or her attitude is when putting can make all the difference. If you think you're going to miss that two-footer, chances are you will. For more on the mental side of putting, I would suggest another book by Dr. Bob Rotella, titled *Putting Out of Your Mind.*

It's been said that putting is as much about art as it is about science, the art being the method that you employ to get the job done. You may have noticed I haven't said anything about the setup, such as the grip, stance, alignment or posture, or many of the other elements in putting, or types of putters. There are so many suggestions in this area, and putting allows for the greatest number and degrees

There are many different styles and preferences when it comes to putting. PGA Tour player Chris DiMarco has a very unique grip (left), Phil Mickelson prefers a very short putter (center), while LPGA star Natalie Gulbis prefers a split-hand grip and a wide, open stance (right).

of stylistic variations. Even the source of power you use (shoulders, arms, or wrists) is a stylistic variation, as are a left-hand-low grip versus a traditional grip, or an open versus square stance. Players can also have preferences such as using a long putter versus a short putter. By observing the top players, you can see the many different putting styles that players employ.

Some putting styles have been made more popular in recent years, as with every era, and the techniques of the past have been put out to pasture. Years ago Hogan, Nicklaus, Palmer, Player, and many of the greatest players in the world putted with a more bent-over posture and mostly powered the stroke with their arms and wrists.

Jack Nicklaus was one of a generation of great putters who employed a then-popular setup of a bent-over posture with the hands close to the body. The stroke was powered primarily by the arms and hands.

Nowadays, the popular putting setup has the player's body lines—feet, hips, shoulders, and forearms—all parallel to the target line. The arms are relaxed and hanging from the shoulders, and the ball is positioned just inside the left heel.

Today, using this method, especially using wrists to power the stroke, is frowned upon. But history shows that these guys scored as well as present-day players; their style and technique couldn't have been that poor, and the conditions of the greens they were putting on were not nearly as good as they are today. With that being said, I'm going to share with you the most commonly used and accepted setup and technique. This method has the player's body aligned: feet, hips, shoul-

With the arms relaxed and hanging, the shoulders, moving up and down in a rocking motion, act as the primary power source in a sense swinging the arms and the putter in a pendulum-type motion.

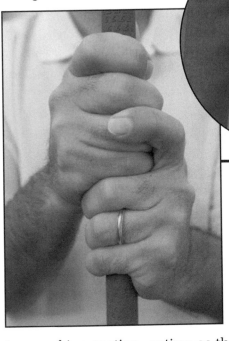

The popular reverse-overlap putting grip. The number of fingers the left pointer finger overlaps on the right hand can vary.

ders, and forearms parallel to the target line, with the ball positioned inside the left heel. The arms hang relatively straight, one of the reasons that shorter putters have become more popular. With the arms relaxed and hanging, the shoulders move up and down in a rocking motion, acting as the power source, in a sense swinging the arms and the putter in a pendulum-type motion. The grip that is commonly used is the reverse-overlap. I personally use a setup similar to this. However, I don't attribute my ability to putt well to this setup, but rather to the fact that I practiced the above exercise with this setup for countless hours over several years. Also, this setup is not set in stone for me. I do go back and forth with my style of putting and from time to time I bend over more, which causes my arms to be bent more at address, and I power the stroke more with my arms and hands than with my shoulders.

All of these setup elements are negotiable, and different ideas and techniques can be found in many books and golf magazines. I suggest you try different styles of these elements, or even a different length putter. A great thing about the putting exercise that I have suggested is you can test different styles of elements to see whether or not a new grip, such as a left-hand-low or the unconventional "claw" grip, a more open or closed stance, a taller or more bent-over posture, or any

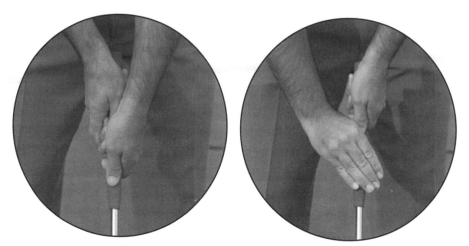

The left-hand-low grip (left) *and the unconventional "claw" grip* (right).

other elements you may want to change or experiment with which may work better for you. You could also use the exercise to see if a longer or shorter putter works better for you. When thinking about elements, don't get too caught up in the "you must do this or that" to be a good putter. Find your own way to do it, even if it's unorthodox. Remember Bill Rockwell, the guy who so successfully putted using only one foot.

To Practice or Not To Practice

When it comes to practice, golfers fall into two categories: those who practice and those who don't. Some golfers don't practice because they don't have time. For those golfers, the good news is that it is possible to get better without practicing, provided they have a clear understanding of the laws of ball flight and the negotiable and nonnegotiable elements of the golf swing. After all, even golfers who don't practice make some changes and adjustments when they hit unacceptable shots. However, those golfers who possess a better understanding of the laws and elements can make more educated choices when making changes. Other golfers find practicing very frustrating, annoying, and a useless waste of time. And it is, if not done correctly. They find it a waste of time because they don't know what to do, what to change, or how to practice. But if they learned how to practice effectively, they could achieve positive results and would probably find practicing a very productive and enjoyable experience. Practicing can be a rewarding experience of discovering new things, conquering challenges, and accelerating the process of improvement.

Golfers who do practice fall into two types: those who practice effectively and improve, and those who practice ineffectively and make little or no progress. Most golfers believe that "practice makes perfect," but this belief is only partially true. I've seen golfers who have played and practiced nearly every day for many years and barely improved, if at all, over this long period of time. I could possibly be one of the greatest examples of this. I spent virtually ten years hitting thousands of balls, but if I were to measure my game before and after this period, I would have to say it was a little better, but not much. By itself, constant practice does not guarantee improvement.

Physically practicing your game can certainly be helpful, but learning has to take place in the mind first, not in the muscles. After you mentally change your understanding and approach to your golf environment, that's when you can work on the physical aspects of changing something in your swing. First, you must understand the relationship between the golf club and golf ball, whether you are working on the long game or the short game. Then, you need to have a good source of feedback. Understanding your ball flight should be the primary source of feedback, but some of the secondary sources I provided in this book can be very helpful and are often needed. You must make a choice about what adjustments to employ to get the ball to produce acceptable results. You can make educated choices or random choices, but possessing understanding can lead to a productive learning environment that allows experimentation and self-discovery to take place.

There are different ways to approach practicing. Repetition is one way. While I believe there are definitely some benefits to constantly repeating a specific motion, it can also have some downsides, depending on the method being used. Some instructors and students believe

that repeating specific drills leads to improvement. I'm not the biggest fan of many drills and exercises. While I do believe in exercises and have provided several in this book, many other exercises that circulate among golfers are not of much use or are absolutely ridiculous. For example, there is the drill, usually pre-

The sensations a golfer feels and the changes that he or she may learn by practicing shots from odd lies, such as a ball above the feet (left), rarely becomes a permanent part of a golfer's swing.

scribed for golfers who slice, that is designed to encourage a shallower, and, thereby, a more inside approach with the club on the downswing. This drill has a golfer hit balls from a lie that has the ball above his or her feet. Because the ball is above the golfer's feet, it requires a flatter, shallower downswing to hit the ball. The question is, where are you going to do this? I doubt your driving range allows you to practice off different types of lies, unless you're at the PGA Learning Center in Port St. Lucie, Florida, the only facility I've ever seen that has this environment available to golfers. But let's assume that you find an area in which to practice hitting balls with the ball above your feet. Will that practice transfer over when you have a normal lie? The one thing that may take place is that you will improve hitting balls from this type of lie. I just don't see the experience transferring over to a normal, flat lie. Another example of this would be to hit balls standing in an unusual position, such as cross-legged, in order to learn better balance. What will most likely happen is that the golfer will learn to have better balance while swinging cross-legged, but once he or she returns to a normal setup, I don't believe what was learned will necessarily transfer over. A golfer must be careful when choosing drills, because many times the sensation and intended change of the drill will not be integrated into their regular swing.

Other drills suggest breaking the movement down into parts, such as taking the club halfway back and checking the position. These types of exercises can be of some benefit, but I believe that doing them over and over again is only somewhat productive at best. The golf swing is a motion and breaking things down into parts just doesn't seem to transfer over into the full motion. Doing them is okay, but I don't recommend repeating them for hours on end with the hope that they'll become permanently integrated into your golf swing.

There are drills or exercises that do enable a golfer to experience a sensation with the club, the body, or both. However, for a drill to be successful, the first thing it needs to do is be applied to improving an element that allows the club to function better. Again, this requires proper diagnosis. Randomly choosing a drill or exercise to help your ball-striking is similar to your being very ill, diagnosing your own sickness, and heading down to the local drugstore. The pharmacist lets you go behind the counter and take all the drugs you want.

Maybe you'll choose one that helps, but you could also choose a medication that does absolutely nothing, makes things worse, or even kills you.

I also believe that hitting ball after ball successively can sometimes produce misleading feedback that gives golfers the impression they're making progress. On the range, the amount of time for most golfers between shots is about 15 to 20 seconds, or about three to four balls per minute. On the golf course, the time between swings is much longer than that, and different clubs are being hit from different types of lies. While practicing, during the short span of time between shots, the brain is working, recalculating adjustments, and making compensations to offset errors. The relatively rapid frequency of hitting shots on the range, compared to the golf course, allows golfers to better sequence and time their actions, thereby creating more desirable results. I see this often at my club. We refer to it as "taking it across the street," because our driving range is on one side of the road and the first tee is across a neighborhood road. Many of our members experience very good results on the range, and then when they get to the first tee, everything changes for the worse.

Golfers don't usually get to practice or warm up on grass because many facilities are too small and it's cost-prohibitive to have a grass range. So courses use the next best thing: artificial turf mats. I've mentioned before that the main problem with mats is that they are much more forgiving than grass is. When the clubhead hits the ground before the ball, the clubhead skips into the ball, many times producing an acceptable result that would be unacceptable if hit on natural grass. When I help golfers who practice on mats, the one source of feedback I have them learn to use is their hearing. When the club strikes the ground before the ball, there is a distinctly different sound than when the ball is struck first. To learn the difference between the sounds, experiment by hitting some short shots with a wedge. If you can learn the sound of when the club strikes the ball first, you can use this feedback to better evaluate the quality of contact at impact.

The market for learning and swing aids has become enormous in the past decade. There are many devices that supposedly will fix your slice, increase your distance, or promise any number of cures for what's ailing your swing. As the saying goes, "If it sounds too good to be true, it probably is." It is understandable that golfers get lured into the idea of these devices being the magic cure. The willingness to try anything is evident when there is a market for golf tees that promise to eliminate the resistance created when the clubhead of a driver hits the tee. Sounds good, but a regular wooden golf tee will create about the same amount of resistance as a bug does when it hits the windshield of your car when you're driving down the highway. Marketers prey on golfers' desires. For many years, I was very much a believer in training aids, both as a player and as an instructor. In fact, at times when I was practicing, I looked like Kevin Costner in the movie *Tin Cup*. In one scene in the movie Costner's character is really struggling with his game and comes walking out of his trailer home with training devices attached all over his head, arms, body, and legs, ready to work on his game. He's willing to try anything to get back his game. I hate to admit it, but in years past I've had some of my students looking like he did in the movie.

I learned an important lesson about learning aids several years back, when I was working on my game. I was focusing on keeping my elbows close together throughout my swing, especially through impact, to improve the solidity of contact. I got one of those devices; in fact, I had a few different ones that wrap around the arms to keep them from separating during the swing. I spent months utilizing this type of device, hitting, without exaggeration, thousands of golf balls. I filmed swings on camera and the results were exactly what I was looking for. But when I took the device off, the results were the same as before: no progress and my arms were still separating. This went on for months. The device worked when I used it, but when I took it off, I was right back where I started. Then, I finally discovered the reason why. The device was doing the work for me. It was keeping my elbows close together, but when there was nothing holding them in place, my arms separated. The lesson I learned from this is that learning aids can be helpful, if they address the correct issue, but they must provide feedback without doing the work for you. After I discovered this, I developed an exercise of hitting balls while trying to keep a foam ball between my arms. I had to do the work to keep the ball between my arms, keeping my elbows close together because if they separated, the ball would fall out. In fact, I actually made a prototype of a device based on this concept, but someone beat me to the marketplace. But that's another story. Learning aids can be useful. In fact, I sell a select group on my website, and sometimes use them with golfers or when working on my own swing. The important thing is to make sure that you have your golf swing issue properly diagnosed, and then find or make something that gives you feedback without doing the work for you.

As I said earlier, I believe the biggest challenge in improving your golf game is that you can't see yourself; and what you feel versus what is really happening are two different things. I can't emphasize this enough. Many times players have to experience what feels like exaggerated movements that are far removed from what they might expect to feel. I see this many times when I work with golfers. For example, maybe a player takes the club too inside on the backswing and it's impacting his or her downswing. We work on the idea of bringing the club straighter back. Often by the time the player gets the club moving the way we want, he or she is in a position that is so far from the original that his or her senses do not allow the player to explore this area. Only through video can I truly get a golfer to believe this. Using video while practicing can be very beneficial, but for most players it's not practical. This is why I strongly recommend the use of a full-length mirror for feedback. It's an invaluable tool for monitoring pre-swing fundamentals and experiencing the golf club in different positions. But you can't bring the mirror to the range. At the range, another set of eyes can be a good source of feedback, and they don't have to belong to a professional. I know I said not to listen to your friends. However, many times I encourage golfers who are taking lessons to bring along someone they play golf with regularly, whether it's a friend or a spouse, to observe the lesson and see what the golfers are doing and what improvements we are trying to make. Even if you don't take lessons, your friends can be very helpful. Earlier I suggested a method for your friends to check your swing plane. If you are educated in your understanding of the golf swing, you can ask them the correct questions to enable them to diagnose what you are or aren't doing in your swing. But before asking the questions, don't assume they know what you are talking about. Show them specifically what you are looking for, whether it is something in your setup or

Objectively look at all aspects of your game from driving to putting, then focus first on practicing the weakest part, perhaps your wedge shots, before practicing the rest.

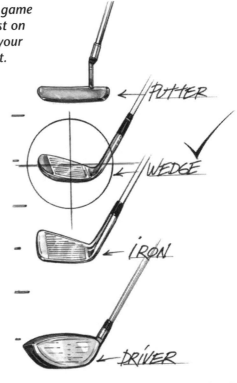

something about the movement of a body part or the golf club when in motion. I'm often amazed at how well people can spot things once they're shown what to look for. On several occasions, I've had my wife, who doesn't really play and has virtually no understanding of the golf swing, watch me hit balls and help me to determine whether I was achieving something particular with my golf swing. Once I showed her what I was doing and what I was trying to do, it was really easy for her to see the difference and act as a second set of eyes for me.

Golf is made up of different games: the long game, the irons, pitching, chipping, bunker play, and putting. Golfers need to break up their practice sessions in order to work on all these different aspects and round out and improve their entire game. A general suggestion is to work on your long game for half of your practice time, and the short game for the other half. Always focus more on the weakest parts of your game. Golfers like to practice what they do well, but practicing what they don't do well is what improves their game. Also practice different types of shots, whether working on your long game or short game. Try to hit some high shots, then hit some low shots, and curve the ball in different directions. Such practice not only helps you build a repertoire of shots for the course, but also allows you to experiment, and in the process, learn different things about the relationship of the golf club to the golf ball.

Regardless of what aspect of your game you are working on, always set goals for each practice session. For example, many golfers find practicing their putting very boring. This is understandable; it's not as exciting as crushing some straight drives on the range. This is why I suggest you set a goal for yourself each time you practice. Not a time goal, meaning that you have to do it for a certain length of time, but rather one that is based on success. Say you decide to do the indoor putting exercise that I suggested earlier. The first day you set a goal of hitting 15 successful putts (shaft lean, center-face hit, etc.), no matter how long it takes. If you hit 15 in a row doing the exercise, you're done for the day. This practice keeps you focused on each putt. As you improve, increase the number of successful putts you need to hit. Or you can start moving farther back, six inches at a time to make the putt longer and more challenging. When you work on your chipping, set a goal for the number of successful chips (contact made with the ground after ball, shaft leaning forward, etc.) that you want to make before moving on to another part of the game. Or with your full swing, the goal could be to successfully hit 20 shots that hook. The idea here is to give your practice session a specific purpose to keep it interesting and effective.

Also, if you are making changes and adjustments while practicing, give the change a chance to produce something consistent. In other words, it may take several swings after making a grip change before you make contact good enough for you to evaluate the change and determine which way you should go with it; more, less, or completely bail on the idea.

The bottom line to effective practice is first to observe the ball flight, whether you are chipping or working on your full swing. Then, determine what the club was doing to produce the ball flight, and improve the movement of the club by itself or through consciously working on a particular element in your swing. While working on the improvement, consider choosing a device, exercise, another set of eyes, or whatever accurate source of feedback that will help you integrate the change. Keep in mind that over time, it's very easy for the feelings of something new to us to dissipate. It's imperative to monitor your changes frequently, as many times we tend to drift back toward "old habits". Practice effectively and your game will improve.

WASHOE COUNTY
LIBRARY SYSTEM
www.washoecountylibrary.us

Items that you checked out

Title: The negotiable golf swing :
ID: 31235035827695
Due: Tuesday, July 2, 2019

Total items: 1
Account balance: $0.00
7/11/2019 11:33 AM
Checked out: 1
Overdue: 0
Hold requests: 0
Ready for pickup: 0

Thank you for using the Washoe County
Library System

CHAPTER 12

Should You Take A Lesson?

Let's start this chapter with a suggestion that all golf professionals love and that golfers often hear: "You need to take a lesson!" Do you, should you, and if so, with whom? All information with regard to golf and the golf swing could be described as lessons. By this definition, lessons are not just something you take with a pro, but rather any experiences in which you have an opportunity to learn. However, I use the term "instruction" to define a lesson with another individual, and in the context of this chapter, a lesson with a golf professional.

A golf professional is someone who receives monetary compensation for helping someone with his or her game. Some professionals belong to golf professional associations. By far the largest, most recognized, and most respected organization in the United States is the PGA, the Professional Golfers Association, an organization of which I have been a member for the past ten years. Just as with any professional organization, be it for doctors, lawyers, writers, or plumbers, there are individuals within their fields who are educated, experienced, qualified, and very competent, and there are others who are not. Golf professionals are no different. There are also golf professionals who are not members of golf associations but who could be qualified and capable of being effective instructors. The questions of who is educated, qualified, and competent are open ended and left to interpretation. The PGA, though, requires the most education to obtain credentials for membership. Along with teaching, its members are required to be trained in many other areas: merchandising, tournament operations, golf car fleet, and turf management, along with many other aspects of business such as accounting, staffing, supervision, and now even restaurant management. Some golf professionals excel, focus, or specialize in these areas. Some only teach and are not responsible for, or involved in, the other aspects of the golf operation at their facilities.

Golfers fall into two categories with regard to taking lessons: those who take them and those who don't. Those who take lessons on a regular basis, or even from time to time, usually find the experience to be helpful, productive, and a valuable source of improvement. Other golfers don't take lessons for various reasons, but I believe mostly because they don't think they need to and believe they can, or want to, figure it out on their own. As I've already stated, humans are problem solvers by nature, and those of you who are parents can witness this by observing your children. My 5-year-old son wants to do everything on his own. He feels he can figure it out. Likewise, trying to unlock what appear to be "the mysteries of golf" is appealing to many.

Other golfers don't take lessons because they are afraid. They've heard that they must get worse before they get better. This is a ridiculous notion. It stems from the facts that incorporating changes can be challenging, the results are not immediate, and golfers sometimes struggle to improve. If nothing else, taking a lesson will hopefully help you better understand your own golf swing, and seeing and understanding your swing can be an epiphany for many golfers and a real turning point in the path to improvement. I often tell golfers I work with that after just one lesson they're on their way to a path of improvement because they better understand their own swing.

Other golfers won't take lessons because they've had a prior bad experience and fear taking lessons again. Bad lesson experiences happen with every instructor at one time or another. Sometimes we don't click with the student. It took me a long time to understand and accept this. The idea that I'm not able to help a golfer is frustrating and disappointing. I consider teaching a tremendous responsibility. People are entrusting me with their games, and paying me good money in hopes that their experience with me can help them to better enjoy their free time playing golf. In some cases, the responsibility is someone's golfing career. I have no better feeling than watching a golfer experience improvement and no worse feeling than a golfer walking off my tee thinking nothing was accomplished. Many times it's a communication issue, or sometimes an instructor is trying to incorporate changes that a golfer is just not capable of doing. Or maybe the student doesn't want to practice and thinks taking a lesson alone is enough to improve his or her game. For these golfers, sometimes golf lessons don't produce positive results.

Let's say you decide you want to take a golf lesson. How do you go about choosing an instructor? Word of mouth is sometimes the best way to get a feel for an instructor before actually going to see him or her. Talk to other golfers who have taken lessons, and ask who they are seeking guidance from. As I already mentioned, there are some instructors who are exceptional professionals and some who are not. Everyone is different, and there are many philosophies and styles of teaching. This is why when it doesn't click with one instructor, you may have to keep trying and find someone who works for you.

Some instructors are labeled method instructors; they teach one method for every golfer or they teach off of the perfect-form swing, or a combination of both. The theories they employ are rigid and non-negotiable. I believe these styles of teaching are ineffective, for reasons that I've already discussed in the book. In my earlier years of teaching, I was a method teacher, one who basically taught off of the model. Like others who teach these methods, I experienced success with some students. But I was not nearly as successful as I am now, tailoring my style to the needs, goals, and talents of the individual golfers I am working with. The method style has been abandoned by some instructors, and I believe the trend will continue to move away from this style of teaching.

If you do decide to take lessons, your expectations need to be realistic. Although much progress can be made through taking lessons, understand that the coach does not make the student. Golf professionals are not magicians and by themselves cannot make you better. Sparky Lyle, the famous baseball coach, once said, "The manager doesn't make the players, it's the other way around. The players make the manager." I have personally experienced this with some of my college players, several of whom I've worked with since junior high school. People say to me that it's unbelievable what I have done with these golfers. But the fact of the matter is that all of the golfers I am privileged to work with have varying degrees of talent, and many times I'm fortunate enough to be able to help them further reach their potential. The student is always the one who makes the changes; the coach is merely the one who provides the guidance. This idea can be illustrated at any level. It's very common for great players to changes coaches, even after they have had successful years with them. A few years ago, when I finally came to this realization, I looked back on those years I plodded along trying to improve. I worked on my own game with many instructors during that time, moving from one to another, trying to see all of the big names. One of the main thrusts of taking lessons from these other pros was to experience different styles of teaching, styles that I could incorporate into my own style. But deep down inside there was another motive: to find the pro who had the secret. I was looking for the magician who could unlock the mystery of golf and the problems in my game, and immediately change my game and my life. Unfortunately, he or she doesn't exist, and it didn't happen.

My view of myself as a teacher, or what I prefer to call a coach, is the role of being a guide to the student, a guide who assists people on their paths to better golf. My style over time has evolved more into a Socratic approach. This approach to learning, named after the philosopher Socrates and made popular by his disciple Plato, incorporates more of a dialogue during the lesson rather than my telling a student what to do. Lessons should be about two people communicating, not just the teacher dictating instructions while the student listens and hopefully understands what the teacher is saying. Teaching gives me an exchange with the golfer, allowing me to find out more about how he or she thinks and learns, and what his or her thoughts are on the golf swing. It involves making the lesson a joint effort between the student and the teacher by coming up with solutions and incorporating them. This is a very common and successfully proven method of teaching in the field of education, but is often not incorporated into golf lessons. It focuses more on creating a learning environment, as opposed to teaching one. One of my more successful experiences was during a lesson when a student needed to change his swing path to a more inside approach. After I explained to him what he needed to change with his swing path, he turned to me and said, "How do I do that?" My response was "I don't know." After seeing his puzzled look, and a moment of silence, I added, "How could you do that?" I was forcing him to think about possible ways of accomplishing the task. He came up with a couple of ideas and then finally struck on one that worked. I really did nothing other than show him what he was doing and what he needed to do. He figured out the solution. Even if the professional you're taking the lesson with does not employ this style, you can benefit from this philosophy by becoming more involved in your lessons. Don't just go to a lesson and try to follow every word and direction of the instructor. Instead, question an instructor or ask why he or she is suggesting you do something. If you don't understand what the instructor is saying, ask him or her to explain it in a different way.

Once you find a professional, and if he or she doesn't ask, explain how often you play, what level you play at, how often you can practice, and what your goals are. An instructor needs to understand your personal goals and the resources you have to reach them, be that physical condition, talent, time, or money, and most likely a combination of all of them. Ask the instructor what his or her favorite golf instructional books are and who influenced his or her philosophies the most. Get at least one of the books and read it so that you can have a better understanding of the golf professional's theory and approach when taking the lesson. It can also help your interaction with the instructor. If he or she doesn't have any favorite books, you may want to run for the car. If possible, bring along someone else that you play golf with to observe your lessons. As I mentioned earlier, he or she can be very helpful in monitoring and helping you incorporate changes. Also, be aware of the type of learner you are. If you are very visual, like most people, you should see someone who employs video in his or her lessons. Video can put golfers in touch with an area and sensation to help them perform a certain motion. The advantage of video is particularly true when learning motor skills, because motor information can be more easily transferred visually than through verbal instruction. Even if you don't respond well to learning through video, I think it's very important for you to be able to see your own swing, at least once, so that you can attach an actual picture of your motion as opposed to the one that's in your mind's eye. If it's your first time seeing yourself, prepare for a possible eye-opening experience.

If you've never taken a lesson and are serious about trying to improve your game, I strongly recommend that you do some research and take a couple of lessons. Don't worry about getting worse before becoming better, or that the instructor will break down your swing and you will have to start all over from scratch (although this could happen). You can always abandon his or her suggested ideas. Dive in and take a few. If you've taken lessons and had a bad experience, try another instructor. I'm confident there are golf professionals who can help on your path to better golf. You just have to find the best one who can help you and your game.

Afterthought

Golf is a wonderful sport that gives us an opportunity to challenge ourselves, the time to enjoy the social aspects of playing the game with family and friends, and the chance to meet people and develop new relationships. For golfers, the experience of playing well brings excitement and joy, even though at other times the game can be equally frustrating and disappointing. One of the reasons many of us are so passionate about the game is the challenge of improving at it, with the possibility of our next round being the best we have ever played. It's a quest that nearly all golfers have.

That quest does not need to be an arduous and torturous task filled with endless hours of hand-bleeding practice and confusion. Rather, it can be achieved through a better understanding of your game, the golf swing, and the reasons that your progress in the past has been slow or nonexistent. You now understand that to reach your goals and improve, you must focus on finding a compatible combination of elements with which to build your golf swing; a golf swing that works for you. You now possess a foundation of understanding from which you can work. You have learned about form and function, ball flight, the elements of direction and distance, and feedback sources that are available to you. Another interesting benefit of acquiring greater understanding and true knowledge is that this can reduce future frustration and increase your ability to deal with poor shots and less than stellar rounds. Although you will still realize that the game is something that can't be mastered, you can now see it as a challenge for a lifetime that can be fun and rewarding, rather than a mystery in which you're forever searching for the magical key to unlock. You've come through the woods and into the clearing; you've come out of the bunker and onto the green.

When I first started writing this book, I had several hopes and reasons for doing it. My main hope was that I would be able to help golfers gain a better understanding, and that the knowledge and observations I presented could become contagious in the golf community and change the way golfers approach the game. But now I realize that my hopes and dreams are more specific than that. I hope that when you pick up the most recent golf magazine with a cover promise for more distance or much lower scores, you'll have the knowledge and understanding that enable you to determine whether what the author is saying is something you should apply to your game to help you improve, or that it doesn't apply to you—it doesn't fit your personal blueprint, or is just another empty promise with little substance—and you'll simply turn the page. I hope you'll gracefully accept that tip from a friend or fellow playing partner, but will know what its value is and whether it's negotiable and worth trying to integrate into your game, or whether it's best to just ignore it. I hope that when you hit a shot, good or bad, you'll have a better understanding of why it happened. My hope is that you now possess the understanding to enable you to realize your full golfing potential.

Index

Nicklaus, Jack, 17, 43, 125, 179

O

Olazábal, José María, 116
one-plane swinger, 80, 84
overlapping, 102

P

Palmer, Arnold, 17, 96, 179
palms, club in, 103–104
Parnevik, Jasper, 96
path, swing, 52–53, 57, 59–61, 63,
    66, 67. *See also* swing plane
  adjustments to, 20, 68–69, 71–72,
    106
  alignment and, 95
  ball position and, 107, 108
  divots and, 148, *149*
  downswing, 76–77
  inside-out, 97, *109*
  outside-in, 92, 97, 109
  in putting, 172, 173, *174*
  right elbow and, 77–79
Peart, Neil, 21
Pelz, Dave, 171, 173, 175
Petaglia, Jim, 106
Pettersen, Suzann, 126
PGA Learning Center, 185
photos, for feedback, 94
Physics of Golf, The (Jorgensen), 68
pivot
  amount of, 121–122
  in bridge swing, 160
  in chip shots, 154–155
  inhibited, *123*, 124
  reverse, 122, *123*
  speed and, 113–114
  stance and, 123
Player, Gary, 179
position
  of ball, 87, 107–109
  in chip shots, 150, 151
  follow-through, 130–131, 142,
    153–157
  in lob shots, *162*, 163
  in pitch shots, 157, *158*

"ready," 88
posture, 87, 88–94, 129–130, 179
Poulter, Ian, *95*
power source, 133–134
  in chip shots, 155
  in downswing, 120
  illusional, 118–120
  lag and, 128
  in pitch shots, 158–159
  in putting, 181
practice, 183–190
pressure, shifting, 116, 130
pre-swing elements, 87–110
Price, Nick, 18, 136, 168
Professional Golfers Association
    (PGA), 191–192
professionals, golf, 191–196
pull, *57*, 61, 68, 96, 98, 100
push, *57*, 95, 100, 109
putter, *189*
putting, 171–182
Putting Out of Your Mind (Rotella),
    178

R

range, driving, 186
repetition, 184
rhythm, 135, 137–140, 142, 143,
    153
right arm thrust, 158
right side system, 75–77
Rockwell, Bill, 171–172, 182
Rotella, Bob, 124, 144, 178
Ruth, Babe, 140

S

sand game, 165–170
Sarazen, Gene, *128*
Schepperle, Abigale, 103
Schepperle, Candace, 103
Schepperle, Dave, 103
Search for the Perfect Golf Swing
    (Cochran and Stobbs), 68
separation, 64–66, 70
setup, 87–110
  for bridge swing, 160

with head down, 32
model, 36–40, 41–43, 44, 45, 47
outside in, 98
pressure during, 105
slowing down your, 136
state of, 34–36
timing of, 135–144
unusual, 42, 43, 45, 46–48, *83, 121, 161*
swing plane, 73–85
Swing the Handle, Not the Clubhead
   (Merrins), 155

T

takeaway, one-piece, 125
target
   alignment with, 94–95, 98, 99
   in chip shots, 150–151, 156
   eyes looking at, 124
   intermediary, 98, 99
tempo, 135–137, *138*, 143
tension
   in arms and wrists, 128
   in chip shots, 155–156
   in hands, 104–105
   thought, conscious, 29, 30, 32, 33, 136
timing, 135–144
transition, between backswing and
   downswing, 130, 137, 143
Trevino, Lee, 43, 96

turf, artificial, 150, 186
two-plane swinger, 80, 84

V

Vardon, Harry, 102
video, for feedback, 91, 94, 188, 193

W

Wadkins, Lanny, 18
weaknesses, focusing on, 189
wedge, *108*, 122, *189*
   on artificial turf, 186
   gap, 157
   pitching, 50, *51*, 66, 150, 156, 157
   sand, 102, 108, 157, *165*, 166
weight
   in bridge swing, 160
   in chip shots, 154, 156
   in pitch shots, 157
   shifting, 116
Witter, Ben, *118*, 119
wood, three, 72
Woods, Tiger, 17–18, 94–95, 125, *128*
wrist(s)
   in chip shots, 152, 153, 154, 155
   in putting, 177, 179, 180
   relaxed, 105, 106
   setting of, 125–126
   during swing, 111, 113, *128*

Praise for THE NEGOTIABLE GOLF SWING

Respected cognitive-science research into the nature of learning anything, even golf, has shown that a teaching, fixing, get-it-right approach to progress is less effective than a learning, developing approach. This reality is at the core of Joe Laurentino's approach to golf instruction and *The Negotiable Golf Swing*, which suggests that golfers stop spending time fixing their golf and start investing time learning to play and learn golf in their own unique way. This can improve a golfer's learning potential, which then improves performance. Joe Laurentino's love of the game of golf and passion for helping golfers can be felt on every page of The Negotiable Golf Swing.

> —Michael Hebron, PGA, MP, CI, *Golf Magazine* and *GolfDigest*
> Top 50 Instructors, 1991 PGA Teacher of the Year, Author of:
> *See and Feel the Inside Move the Outside, The Art and Zen of
> Learning Golf, Golf Swings: Secrets and Lies,* and *Golf Mind,
> Golf Body, Golf Swing.* www.MichaelHebron.com.

I have known Joe Laurentino for over 30 years. We grew up at the same public golf course. We both love this game. His passion for his craft shows through in this wonderful book, in which he's clearly done his homework. If you're interested in clear, concise and fundamentally sound information that will in fact make you a better player, *The Negotiable Golf Swing* is the read for you.

> —Tom Patri, PGA, *Golf Magazine* Top 100 Instructor, author of
> *The Six-Spoke Approach to Golf: A Blueprint for Success.*
> www.TomPatri.com

Read this book, it will help you understand what the clubface is doing while in motion, what's important in hitting a golf ball, and why the golf ball flies the way it does. The explanation in *The Negotiable Golf Swing* of the movement of the right arm and right shoulder in the downswing is the best I've ever read.

> —David Glenz, PGA, *Golf Digest* Top 50 and *Golf Magazine*
> Top 100 Instructor, 1998 PGA Teacher of the Year, author of
> *Lowdown from the Lesson Tee: Correcting 40 of Golf's Most
> Misunderstood Teaching Tips.* www.DavidGlenz.com

Credits

AP Images: Pages 45, 46 (center), 79, 88 (middle, bottom), 112 (bottom right), 120, 124, 128 (top center), 140, 151 (#1, #2, #3, #4), 161 (top center), 164, 170, 179 (top left, top center, top right, bottom right), 133 (top left, top right, bottom left, bottom right).

David Cruickshanks: Page 48

Getty Images: Pages 46 (top), 81 (top right), 112 (#2, bottom left, bottom center), 172,

Golf Magazine: 126 (top left, top center)

Historic Golf Photos: Pages 112 (#1),

Leonard Kamsler; Pages 43, 65, 78 (top left, top center), 82 (bottom center, bottom right), 96, 100 (bottom center, bottom right), 112 (#3, #4, #5, #6, #7), 116 (top right), 121 (bottom center, bottom right), 125 (bottom left, bottom center), 128 (bottom left), 130 (bottom left, center, right)

Mark Newcombe: Pages 76, 78 (middle left, bottom center, bottom right), 80 (top left, middle), 81 (bottom center, bottom right), 82 (top left, middle left), 85, 93, 95, 112 (#8), 116 (top center), 117, 127, 128 (top right), 141, 161 (top right, middle right)

Charles Voorhees: 174 (top left and right), 175

All other interior photos, including jacket flap, by Robert Walker and are the property of Joseph Laurentino.

Cover photo by Jim Lennon

All illustrations, including back cover, by Phil Franke.